ZEN AND CHRISTIAN

ZEN and CHRISTIAN

The Journey Between

John Dykstra Eusden

Crossroad · New York

1981
The Crossroad Publishing Company
575 Lexington Avenue, New York, NY 10022

Library of Congress Cataloging in Publication Data

Eusden, John Dykstra.
Zen and Christian, the journey between.

Includes index.
1. Zen Buddhism—Relations—Christianity,   2. Christianity and other religions—Zen Buddhism.   I. Title.
BQ9269.4.C5E97   294.3'927   81-7837
ISBN 0-8245-0099-7   AACR2

For Andrea, Alan, Dykstra, and Sarah—
in all their journeys

Contents

Gratitude and *Gassho*

To my wife Joanne—for her sense of expression, which helped to recast each chapter, and for her encouragement.

To American and Japanese colleagues who read parts of the manuscript or listened to its unfolding (being told, perhaps, more than they wanted to hear)—for their criticism and their support:

Alice and Otis Cary, Paul B. Courtright, Peter K. Frost, Philip Kapleau, J. Thomas Leamon, H. Ganse Little, Jr., William F. May, Carl R. Samuelson, Mark C. Taylor, Laura and Robert Fukada.

Abe Masao, Araki Michio, Doi Masatoshi, Hisamatsu Shin'ichi, Nishitani Keiji, Shimano Eido, Takeuchi Yoshinori, Yamada Hisashi.

To Sybil-Ann Sherman for checking and typing—time after time, with spirit and humor. And to Rosemary Lane and Donna Chenail for help at the end.

Kyoto, Japan
Randolph, New Hampshire
Williamstown, Massachusetts

Ganjin, a blind Chinese monk
in zazen or meditation posture.

One

MORE THAN ONE THING

As I put on the light,
More plum-flowers are seen behind
Branches fair and white.

Gyodai

The earth is the Lord's, and the fullness thereof,
The world, and those who dwell therein.

Ps. 24:1

New possibilities

It was dawn and the sitting had begun. A short while before, we had finished cross-country skiing under the three-quarter moon, trying to work silently on rhythm and pattern in our movements across a field full of light. Now the moment of concentration and no movement had come as we began zazen—the time of cross-legged, straight-back posture, of counting breaths, exhalations and inhalations, of thoughts arising and fleeing. Darkness gave way to grayness and then to the whiteness of a bright January day; one phase was naturally leading to another, and a similar sequence was repeated in the sitting. Soon I was able to follow my breathing "with my mind's eye," not having to count the movements of my abdomen in the deep, centered, slight activity of my body. Then I felt no longer apart from the people sitting with me, no longer apart from other people, close to things like snow and trees, joined to the floor, unmindful of time and its passage. I felt, as Zen people say, that I had reached a good "place." As we drank green tea after the sitting, continuing silence, or listening, or at times speaking, I mentioned Nishida Kitaro's poem:

> There's something bottomless
> Within me, I feel.
> However disturbing are the waves
> Of joy and sorrow,
> They fail to reach it.[1]

It was late in Advent, and the joy of Christmas was beginning to encircle. The carillon rang through the cold night as people filled the chapel, now at its best with candles giving warm light to great stone walls, making the sanctuary a special place to be. On this night of a traditional Lessons and Carols Service, the choir began singing softly, as a processional, "Once in royal David's city stood a lowly cattle shed, where a mother laid her baby . . . . He came down to earth . . . and his shelter was a stable and his cradle was a stall. With the poor and mean and lowly lived on earth our Saviour holy." An exultant crescendo swelled as the procession reached the front of the chapel with the organ and hundreds of voices joining in—it was as if the Christmas spirit had now descended, and everyone sensed the presence of "something other" and the offering of renewal and joy. As I processed with the choir, I thought of Friedrich Schleiermacher's words about Christmas eve: "The solemn wrinkles are for once smoothed away; the years and cares do not stand written on the brow. Eyes sparkle and dance again." [2]

Zen and Christian. Two experiences—so different,

rooted in cultures and histories worlds apart. And yet each has an authenticity for me, and each lays a claim on me. The sitting and the Advent service were hardly isolated happenings, but have occurred in kind over and again. Those from the East are relatively new, coming through Zen discipline and practice, *sutra* or scripture study, and teaching history of religions for more than two decades in Japan and America. The Christian experiences have always been there—beginning with earliest memories of liturgical and biblical drama in the Congregational church of my childhood, known in my father's preaching, nurtured by graduate work with H. Richard Niebuhr, confirmed by association with the ecumenical Taizé Community in France and America, and continued by writing and teaching about the Puritans and American religious thought. And now the two are mixed and each a part of me.

Perhaps the mixture is not so strange. We live in a planetary world, no longer rigidly set off by physical factors and no longer dominated by provincial ways. Even in the heretofore most rigorously separated areas, startling changes are occurring. The dialects of the Chinese language sprang up because people of one river valley literally did not know—and had no possibility of knowing—those of the other river-valley systems. The riparian subcultures of China are breaking up, but so are the rigidities of the whole world. Given the new situation of the late twentieth century, Arend T. van Leeuwen offers these words: "Now that the unity of mankind is something actually within our purview, we simply must be up-to-date enough to bring the *whole* world into *all* of our thinking."[3] In the realm of religion this means not just toleration, not mere acceptance. Our space-time nearness to other cultures offers us the chance to learn genuinely from others. Phrases such as "cross-fertilization" and "the unity of an orderly conversation"—in itself a fundamental learning process in the study of world religions—can be attested to in the experiences of many of us and confessed to be factors which mold our lives and religious values. New possibilities urge us to leave behind our own relativities, so often made into absolutes, in order to continue our quest for an understanding of self and of the world.

A wider meaning of religion

Many Westerners have found meagerness in their present religious surroundings and have traveled elsewhere. A religion must have what Paul Tillich calls "a dimension of depth," and I find, with a great company, such a dimension often lacking in contemporary representations of Christianity. There are, happily, exceptions. Yet, much of the preaching, art, uses of space, liturgy, and structure of "public worship" in today's Christian life do not always point to an illuminating truth, to an interpretive principle, to a ground of being, to a supreme quality of life, or to a hope. Christian forms and practices obscure and twist the meaning and power of the gospel. I think, for example, of a modern statue of Christ erected in front of a church administrative building in Washington, D.C.—a statue I passed and wondered about while on a daily journey of cycling to work. The figure of Christ is several stories high, made of a burnished material, set on a tall pedestal constructed of the same kind of concrete used for the walls and the tight little window frames behind it. The right hand of Christ is raised with palm thrusting toward the viewer. The lines of the casting are square and angular. The statue is foreboding, but more likely, at least to me, judgmental and even condemning. The title of the statue is *I Am the Light of the World*. The left hand clasps a scroll identified as Isaiah 9, the chapter of those unparalleled words of assurance and covenant: "The people who walked in darkness have seen a great light." What a contrast between the words referred to and the form of the statue! The illumination and compassion of Christ were difficult to discern as I would look up twice a day and return again, unmoved, to my pedaling through traffic.

A spiritual journey is also made by many of us because we see religion in a wider scope than did our parents and grandparents. Some of us would say that our present way of viewing religion is even different from our conception a few years ago. I, at least, am no longer able to think of religion as somehow being equated with "revelation," or totally deducible from biblical theology. Nor do I sense that I am proclaiming religious truth, in some comprehensive fashion, when I am learnedly speaking Christian "God language." Religion in our planetary world is a larger, more mysterious, more fascinating subject than we have heretofore allowed it to be.

Not only are present-day Western Christians involved in this search for something wider, but Easterners are adding their own impetus and imagination to the venture. For many Zen people, the quest for the meaning of religion overflows and passes beyond—in the water symbolism of the Tao—the traditional vessels of the *dharma,* the Buddhist law; the *sangha,* the religious community; the *sutras,* the scriptures; and even the discipline of zazen, or meditation. For some Buddhists today, the new force of religion in its flow touches and surrounds some of the teachings of the West, including those of the gospels.

The new understanding is not so new if we think of the Western philological origins of "religion." The word is partly connected with the Latin *religare,* to "bind," to "tie down," to "fasten"—and many have always taken this derivation as central, stressing a normative conception of religion. But religion is also derived from the Latin word *rele-gere,* which means primarily to "put back against," or to "lay back against." In a specific, literal sense the word, among Roman mariners, meant to "furl," the tying back of the sail against the boom or mast in heavy weather while on an open-sea journey. In later philosophical and literary refinements, *relegere* had the sense of "traveling through again," or of "finding a background," or "placing things in perspective." In Roman literature and among certain medieval and Reformed Christian thinkers, a conception or a practice was religious when, first of all, it was like the proper backdrop on a stage, providing range and depth to the acting and the objects in front. I prefer this perspectival meaning offered by *relegere.* Religion is that which links together and gives sense to seemingly scattered and even contradictory experiences and phenomena. Religion is related to human life through the giving of meaning to the multiple realities confronted in the culture of any age.

Most important in a present understanding of religion is the attention now being given to symbols. Religion, like all cultural phenomena, functions through the use of symbols. Discussion about the meaning of the word *symbol* abounds, but let it be said briefly that a symbol is a particular practice, art form, historic event, ideal type, relation which points to and can encapsulate central concepts, norms, hopes, desires, goals. Or a symbol is something specific which has the power to project and illuminate an interpretive and controlling idea.

For Christians, the symbol above all others which gives meaning to human history and culture is the cross. It may be interpreted as that which points generally to the significance and message of the heroic life of one who gave himself for others; or, in a more literal understanding, it may be seen rooted in the ground as a vivid and convincing reminder of God's presence in history, reconciling the world in all of its ambiguities to divine love and providence. Other symbols will be important, too, for Christians: a stable, crowded by those of low and high estate, wherein promises are proclaimed; the figure of the shepherd-savior, known to be one who searches for that which is lost; a tomb, first sealed and then opened and empty. For the Confucian, the primary symbol would be the representation of the good son—the one who so knows the meaning of the *li,* the rites, that they are in him naturally like the grain in bamboo or the markings in jade. The faithful son is not one who just performs slavish obedience; he is rather the one who understands that self-abnegation and a compassionate relationship to others produce completeness and a sense of vital function. For Zen what would a central symbol be? Perhaps it would be the circle which adorns teachers' and monks' robes and is often found in large iron or wood forms in temples, signifying the Zen stress on unity or "something total." Or it might be one of the many brush and ink paintings of Bodhidharma, the first Zen "patriarch," known as a man of composure, determination, and even fierceness. For me and many others, it would be the ancient carving of the blind monk Ganjin, sitting in zazen posture; he appears completely natural and reposed—yet solid and concentrated, implying a sense of being joined not only to the floor but also to the rest of what he considers reality.

We are caught up in our symbols, be they Christian, Confucian, Zen or rooted in American "secular religion." We may simply accept the symbols given to us, or we may struggle with them, and, on rare occasions, we may make new ones. But we must have them in order to be human. Our species can rightly be known as *homo symbola habens*—a being who has symbols—or, in more creative times, *homo symbola faciens*—a being who makes symbols. Symbols illumine human destiny; they give us self-understanding; they guide our decisions; they help give us power to act; and they inform the basis of our relations to others. We are emotionally attached to them. In my understanding of religion, symbols, if they are genuinely religious, must do one thing more—and here I part company with many who see religion only as a part of culture. Symbols will relate people to some ultimate reality, such as love for the Christian, wisdom for the Confucian, or unity and connectedness for the Zen person. Religion deals in its symbols with some quality, some purpose, some affirmation which is of ultimate significance. Although religion always exists within a culture and carries the marks of that culture in any statement of its perspective, it finally points to something that transcends that culture. The meaning of Christian love is not only known to Westerners; Confucian wisdom is sought beyond China; and Zen unity is pursued in New York and California. Perhaps the cross, the good son, and the circle come "from the collective unconscious and its integration with the conscious mind";[4] perhaps they are still only the ultrafine projections of our cultural conditioning—crowning, so to speak, the given data of different cultural experiences. Perhaps they are personal, private attempts at a "game" of symbolic self-transcendence. While not excluding the insight of such assertions about religious symbols, I would say that such symbols exist because of the mysterious reaction of people in their culture with an ultimate reality—something that is related to the human mind and imagination as well as to social and economic structures, but is not totally deducible from either humankind or culture. I subscribe to such a possibility and would use the word *sacred* to describe a primordial reality—whether known as love, wisdom, unity, emptiness, or something else—and say that religion is concerned with the search for meaningful symbols to express such reality.

What can be said of the religious person—he who is attempting to lead a life in perspective, interpreting and finding symbols of intellectual and emotional power, and striving to accord with a subtending value or purpose? What are his marks? To be sure, as a religious person, he might be vindictive, warlike, punitive, as history has so often demonstrated: Christian crusaders sacking Constantinople, medieval Buddhist sects warring in Japan, nineteenth-century American Christians defending slavery, twentieth-century Hindus battling Muslims. But if we were to speak of the ideal, admitting aberrations and contaminations, we might refer to Paul's list of the "fruit of the Spirit" in Galatians 5:22–23. The religious person is one who possesses and in some way manifests "love, joy, peace, patience, kindness, goodness, faithfulness, gentleness, self-control." Christian, Taoist, Sufi, Confucian, Jew, Zen could all say that these are qualities of the religious person, no matter how often they have been forgotten or debased.

Today many of us would add to Paul's list, especially if there has been a journey to the East. Additional fruit might be simplicity, beauty, wonder, and the body. If one is engaged in the wider meaning of religion, one is not content today with the cerebral and often superficial spiritual life which characterizes much of Western theology and worship. Most branches of the Christian church have failed to take seriously the place of feelings and emotions, although the emphases of Augustine, Saint Francis, the medieval mystics, and Jonathan Edwards are waiting for us in our tradition. Contemporary Christian theologians have generally found it difficult to understand the place and influence of the unconscious depths. Mircea Eliade has written about our need of bringing to the surface that which is buried in our inmost depth, especially the longing for a whole and regenerated life, much as primitive people express and fulfill in rites of initiation and association and in the celebration of seasons.

So a new, but also old, meaning of religion has caught up many of us. In looking for a wider perspective that will allow us to grasp the possibilities of our world, in our need for and attachment to life-explaining and life-giving symbols, and in our quest for new fruit of the spirit, we are crossing religious boundaries and journeying to other traditions. This book speaks of my attraction to Zen as a Christian and the meaning of the relationship of the two perspectives in me—or of my ongoing "journey between." The crossing over to Zen is not done to gain some new base of certainty, but rather in the hope of "attaining insight and understanding," as the Roman Catholic writer John Dunne says, and thereby gaining a sense of personal integration and function.[5] The book has less to do with Christianity than with Zen, for it is primarily addressed to those who stand in the Judeo-Christian tradition and wonder about the possibility of looking beyond to other concepts and ways.

Perhaps it is the extension of Paul's fruit of the spirit that I find most appealing in Zen—the involvement of the whole person in an expression of what we know ourselves to be and in what we feel must yet be discovered. A colleague in the Christian ministry, one who has assisted in a concentrated course in Zen discipline, especially in his field of art, wrote these words: "Zen has a wholeness. It seems to me so accessible and tangible, perhaps operational, in common practice. The harmonious yet paradoxical blend of humor and deep seriousness, of whimsey and profound philosophical exploration, of art and sport, body and spirit seems so much more pervasive than our remote theorizing and our often feeble attempt to combine the spiritual and the intellectual. Where in our brand of religion is there anything like the concrete discipline of the whole being, the working with the person in the entirety of personhood?" [6]

The appeal is so understandable in an enlarged conception of religion. Zen—with its genuineness, search for true Mind, quiet, and action. Or as the qualities of seventeenth-century Basho,[7] perhaps the most memorable of the *haiku* poets, have been described: "A desire to use every instant to the uttermost; a feeling that nothing is alone, nothing unimportant; a wide sympathy; and an acute awareness of relationships of all kinds, including that of one sense to another." [8]

Boundaries—changing, yet needed

But still . . . Zen *and* Christian. I am what I am and, no matter how influential the journey, no matter how great the enlargement of my understanding about religion, I remain Western and Christian. There has been a chance to look and compare—to "try the spirits" in other realms. But I am claimed by and I am always reappropriating the social concern of the Christian ethic, the winsome figure of Jesus in the Synoptic Gospels, the startlingness of the Word made flesh, the never-ending Christian probe into the meaning of love, and the proclamation of man's need for community.

Even if such matters in Christianity did not attract me, a journey to the East could hardly lead to permanent spiritual residence. The chance of a Westerner getting totally inside the Zen way is remote. Gary Snyder, the American poet who tried and succeeded as well as any, speaks of just the language problem: "We who have studied Zen in Japan have had to master Japanese or get as good at it as we could, to learn to read Chinese in the Japanese manner so that we could translate our own koan [a short, jolting question for use in meditation], and also follow the roshi's teisho [lectures]. So there is a tremendous amount of just slogging around in language work for us, as well as sitting, and there have never been very many people who have stuck it out long enough to do this . . . generally the people who stay a year or so just barely scratch the surface of Rinzai practice." [9] I think of the many years Eugen Herrigel had to spend in Japan before he could write *Zen and the Art of Archery,* which deals with only one phase of the discipline. Harvey Cox has written realistically and sensitively about wider problems in *Turning East: The Promise and Peril of the New Orientalism.*

But suppose a Westerner does manage the language, does find a master or roshi with whom she has *innen,* or rapport and relationship, and does spend long periods of time, spread over the years, in Japan—or at Tassajara Zen Center in California—what then? Sooner or later she faces a truth: That from which she has come never leaves her.

Even though I say I transcend my culture in a commitment to Zen, I nonetheless take my Western ways with me. They are more than inseparable baggage; they form the life web upon which are suspended many of my values, my forms of action, my responses, my likes and dislikes. My cultural positioning is undeniable in its force and influence. Even when I say I choose or rechoose Christianity, the process of "choosing" is complicated and ambiguous. It certainly is not an act of pure voluntarism. I choose, but I carry much with me in my act of choosing from the place, the family, the body politic, the history in which I have been placed. As Alfred Schutz, the Austrian sociologist and philosopher, puts it: "This world is always given to me . . . . I was, so to speak, born into this organized social world and I grew up in it. Through learning and education, through experiences and experiments of all kinds, I acquire a certain ill-defined knowledge of this world." [10]

So it is with Christianity—now affirmed, now qualified, but never forgotten. It is a part of me: I have never left it and I return to it, no matter what my journey. Like Odysseus landing in his homeland of Ithaca, I might ask upon return, "Whose country have I come to now? . . . If only I had stayed there with the Phaeacians!" [11] But there is no staying out there. Ernst Troeltsch says about Christianity and those upon whom it makes a claim: "Only through [Christianity] . . . have we become what we are. . . . Thus we are and thus we shall remain, as long as we survive. . . . Christianity has grown up with us and has become a part of our being." [12] In thinking about my journey I would echo Troeltsch's words and say, at least, that Christianity has grown up with me—or, rather, I with it.

So, Christian as well as Zen, by choice but also by having had a history and therefore being where I am.

In today's quest for self-understanding, is it so odd that a person is claimed by two things? Because of new social and psychic forces and because of what we are now asking about ourselves, we no longer come neatly packaged and identified. Many of us have come to know that the search for personal identity—in its genuineness and in its frequently brutal force—is largely connected with the desire and the need to escape the notion of fixity. The women's liberation movement is telling members of both sexes such a message. William James rightly identified in his decades-old *Principles of Psychology* the "sub-universes" of our existence and experience. For each one of us, as

Schutz writes, "there exist several, probably an infinite number of various orders of reality, each with its own special and separate style of existence . . . the frontiers of reality are gliding." [13] Modern folk are no longer totally blocked off from things that they might become—by river valleys, by parental conditioning, by roles thrust upon them, by the Christian scriptures, or by Zen practice.

Our potential does not, however, call for the elimination of boundaries. [14] Who can live without knowing and proclaiming what one is in distinction to what one is not—without a sense of some things being "set"? As Paul Tillich has said, "[A] frontier is not only something to be crossed . . . boundary is a dimension of form, and form makes everything what it is." [15] To break down all boundaries so that a person is not at home within certain spheres and has no sense of identity is to live in a "pseudo-instinctualism," governed by ebb-and-flow whimsey and a chaotic sense of personal history. We live not only in disorder, but also in loneliness and ultimately in isolation, if we are without boundaries—whether one is thinking of marriage and the family, or of vocation, or of a workable image of self to have in one's own mind or to present to others. Both Zen and the Christian faith are forces which have the power of creating workable, useful delineations. Participants in each of these religious perspectives are urged to define themselves as being grasped by a history and development stretching back two and three millennia.

The problem is not to eliminate boundaries, but to understand their place and to know what is happening to them and to ourselves. We cannot return to an age when limits were conceived as inviolate, and laws governing human actions and aspirations were thought to be fundamental and unchanging—no matter how beckoning such a "golden time" might appear in retrospect, or in our despair. Today we all face the erosion and destruction of previous boundaries and the perplexing task of finding and re-creating new boundaries and limits for our existence.

The new boundaries we are fashioning for ourselves do not neatly interlock or form symmetrical patterns. How does one put together the Christian, biblical concern for a "God who acts in history" with the Zen points of "no god" and emptiness? Or how does one juggle the Christian, Western stress on parts and duality—man and God, sin and grace, law and gospel, matter and form, cause and effect—with the contrary Zen notion of unity and nonduality? Perhaps a beginning answer is: Don't aim at any easy fitting together of the parts. It's more important to be a full person and to find out what can help you break out of moribund, life-denying boundaries than it is to put yourself into some clearly labeled, tight package. Being full may involve being several different and distinct things.

Ernst Troeltsch pointed out that we must engage in the difficult task of grasping the way in which the "Divine Life," as he stated it, manifests itself. The divine life does not refer to the "mind of God," or a similar doctrine, but rather to the broader concept of the meaning of human possibility. The divine life is not known in any consistent development or logical presentation of an absolute position, but in "always-new and always-peculiar individualizations." We grasp the unfolding of the divine life in "the fulfillment of the highest potentialities of each separate department of life." [16] To give heart, mind, eye, ear, touch to the new which bursts out in the ground of our lives—and to nurture it—is to take beginning steps toward being not only a full person but also a religious person.

But how is this to happen? One way is to begin where we are. Another way, to be discussed at the end of the book, is to understand that a true knowledge of ourselves can occur in the presence of and through the opposite of what we happen to be at any moment. This chapter closes with the first way. The moving across boundaries to be at home in other realms can result when we plumb thoroughly and imaginatively one area and discover trans-forming insight and energy. Consider the psychological quest for a workable, integrated self. The power of therapy, involving both theory and application, is the power of self-transformation. I am speaking of the work engaged in by both patient and therapist in psychoanalysis as well as the hard process of honest self-reflection. The transformation that comes with a rigorous journey into the self is not easy and the coming back no less difficult. But, as Yeats has said,

> Nothing can be sole or whole
> That has not been rent.[17]

When I accept a seeming nothingness about myself, there can emerge, even in despair, a sense of wonder about what will happen and a sense of anticipation. I become some-thing else—set free—when I come to understand the his-tory, agony, and depth of myself. If the process works, I can grasp transforming power, and be led beyond my for-mer self-understanding and mode of operation and across previously impenetrable boundaries.

So it is in the closely connected field of religious experi-ence. To go down into the depths of zazen practice or into the discipline of the rule of the Christian Taizé Community—to plumb deeply one thing—is to come back up as a new person. The religious journey "down into" is accompanied, like the psychological, with questioning, doubt, and anguish. The affirmation of the religious way, going beyond the psychological, is that down in the enclaves of an intense experience—again, if the process works—it is possible to discover the changeable, shatterable self in the presence of something "other." There can be a meeting with something that does not change, break, or fade. I may be able to encounter the Spirit of lights "with whom there is no variableness or shadow of turning" (James 1:17) or that eternal reality, "unchanging, standing as One, unceasing. . . . I do not know its name and call it Tao" (*Tao Te Ching,* chap. 25). I come back with forceful energy, breaking out of Apollonian inheritances and structures, ready for the newness of many possibilities. The gospels portray Jesus as one propelled from the depth of his spiritual experience to new things; he calls us to do the same. A Zen master is likewise propelled, and he urges his students to break forth. Genuineness and intensity in one thing can lead not to narrowness, but to comprehension and understanding of many things. Transformation known as self-transcendence is a genuine religious direction. Perhaps it may be said that the ability to go on to things once not even conceived—to cross boundaries—is the measure of the depth and the quality of what I have discovered where I am. It is true that it is possible to be Buddhist for Christian reasons, and vice versa.

I have a friend in New York City who is a tea master as well as a Zen practitioner. In the midst of the rush, the tension, the smog of the metropolis, he follows his profession of tea ceremony, offered to all interested persons, at the United Nations Plaza on the East River. The ceremony is authentic, concentrating on the naturalness of drinking tea, silence, the sense of sharing, and the esthetics and "just nowness" of the moment—all of which are central to the Zen spirit. I have always been deeply moved when my students and I have participated with him in this centuries-old art and discipline. The tea master has often spoken to us about the rigors of training, his sense of being set free by the ceremony, and his consequent readiness to understand and attempt new things. One day a Roman Catholic priest friend asked him to do a tea ceremony during the celebration of mass in the priest's church. At first the tea master demurred. How could the two possibly be done together? Would he and his priest friend be able to share these deep moments from their different traditions? What would the meaning be for those who came to the "tea-ceremony mass"? But he said yes, in Zen awareness of all things—and in response to the courage and openness of his friend.

He discovered that the mass and tea ceremony had much in common: Each presented a flow and development of liturgy and each required the participation of those present in physical acts of deep significance. Each had a history of change in procedure and in symbolic structure. And yet the two were different. As for his own feelings, the tea master reported that he knew it was good to be there; he did not feel strange. What was the basis of his positive response? He was a tea master and remained so during the mass, just as his friend remained a priest during the passing of the bitter green tea and the sweet biscuit. Interpenetration of meaning was possible because each art was being pursued in its own genuine way. There was and could be no simple combination of each—or cheap eclecticism. The authentic performance of each act in the presence of the other was an illuminating and provocative experience. The tea master reported that he had known little about Roman Catholicism before, but that after the intense experience of performing his exact art in the chancel of the church, he was ready to respond to the other liturgy and to learn more. Thorough, never-easily-gained participation in your own way and art can lead to a beginning comprehension of another. To really know tea may open you to an understanding of bread and wine, as well as the reverse.

So today, for many reasons we are not only one thing. An expanding mobile age, a wider conception of religion, a search for new "fruit of the spirit," a different sense of boundaries, and an interpenetration resulting from making a true plumb of one's own way are leading us out from confinements and even imprisonments. As my tea-master friend says, "Potentially we can be many things."

Notes

1. Trans. Suzuki Daisetz in William Johnston, *The Still Point: Reflections on Zen and Christian Mysticism* (New York: Fordham University Press, 1970), p. 46.

2. Friedrich Schleiermacher, *Christmas Eve: Dialogue on the Incarnation,* trans., intro., notes Terrence N. Tice (Richmond: John Knox Press, 1967), p. 85.

3. Arend T. van Leeuwen, *Christianity in World History: The Meeting of the Faiths of East and West,* trans. H. H. Hoskins, foreword D. H. Kraemer (New York: Charles Scribner's Sons, 1964), p. 427. His italics.

4. Carl G. Jung, *Two Essays on Analytical Psychology,* trans. R. F. C. Hull (New York: Meridian Books, 1965), p. 96.

5. John Dunne, *The Way of All the Earth: Experiments in Truth and Religion* (New York: Macmillan, 1972), p. 44.

6. Letter from the Rev. J. Thomas Leamon, Jan. 30, 1970.

7. No diacritical marks are used in Japanese, Chinese, or Sanskrit words—the book being intended for the general reader. E.g., Bashō becomes Basho and kōan becomes koan. Also, in order to produce continuity for the eye, the great number of Japanese words dealing with Zen practice have not been italicized, e.g., roshi (master or teacher), zendo (meditation hall), zazen (meditation). Chinese and Japanese names are rendered family name first and given name second.

8. Harold G. Henderson, commentary and trans., *An Introduction to Haiku: An Anthology of Poems and Poets from Basho to Shiki* (Garden City: Doubleday, 1958), p. 21.

9. Gary Snyder, "On Rinzai Masters and Western Students in Japan," *Windbell* 8, nos. 1, 2 (Fall 1969): 23.

10. Alfred Schutz, *Collected Papers,* vol. 2, *Studies in Social Theory,* trans. and ed. Arvid Brodersen (The Hague: M. Nijhoff, 1964), p. 9.

11. Homer, *The Odyssey* (New York: Penguin Books, 1967), p. 207.

12. Ernst Troeltsch, "Relativism: The Place of Christianity among the World Religions," in *Attitudes toward Other Religions: Some Christian Interpretations,* ed. Owen C. Thomas (New York: Harper & Row, 1969), pp. 10, 79.

13. Schutz, *Collected Papers,* 2:135, 148.

14. Robert J. Lifton, *Boundaries: Psychological Man in Revolution* (New York: Random House, 1970); Peter L. Berger, *Facing Up to Modernity: Excursions in Society, Politics, and Religion* (New York: Basic Books, 1977); Robert N. Bellah, *Beyond Belief: Essays on Religion in a Post-Traditional World* (New York: Harper & Row, 1970); David L. Miller, *The New Polytheism: Rebirth of the Gods and Goddesses* (New York: Harper & Row, 1974); James A. Ogilvy, *Many Dimensional Man: Decentralizing Self, Society, and the Sacred* (New York: Oxford University Press, 1977).

15. Paul Tillich, *The Future of Religions,* ed. Jerald C. Brauer (New York: Harper & Row, 1966), p. 57.

16. Troeltsch, "Relativisim," in *Attitudes,* p. 79.

17. William Butler Yeats, "Crazy Jane Talks with the Bishop," *The Collected Poems of W. B. Yeats* (New York: Macmillan, 1933), p. 298.

Two

WHAT IS ZEN?

> Be master of the situation
> Wherever you may find yourself.
>
> *Rinzai*

> With your help I leap over a bank,
> by God's aid I spring over a wall.
>
> *2 Sam. 22:30*

Impossible to speak, but . . .

Whoever writes anything about Zen is under the judgment of a seven-character expression which reads, "The instant you speak about a thing, you miss the mark." Warnings over definition, argument, and verbalization belong, in large part, to the influential Taoist inheritance of Zen Buddhism. The Taoist-Zen point of view reminds us that we cannot rest with neat phrases and logical delineations. "Words are the fog one has to see through," as one saying puts it.

Western scholars of religion, unlike many of their Chinese and Japanese colleagues, have usually had a love affair with words and language. It is difficult for most Westerners to think that a concept cannot be made more clear by speaking of it or a contrast made more useful by a careful drawing of nuances. We have generally "tended to assume that an elegant verbal solution to a problem would suffice to settle it."[1] And for that assumption we should heed the Zen critique. But we do attach, with some reason, great productivity and creativity to words. As W. H. Auden says, "Language is the mother, not the handmaiden of thought; words will tell you things you never thought or felt before."[2]

This chapter is presented with *innen,* or rapport with and feeling for, the Zen insistence on "no words."

> The wind is soft, the moon is serene.
> Calmly I read the True Word of no letters.[3]

It is also offered in the hope that something can and should be said, and that in the telling—and perhaps in the reading—matters will be the more understandable. For one can become overly attached to "no letters." Zen teachers have traditionally said that silence *and* speech are needed and that neither can supplant the other. A saying puts it, "Thirty blows, though you can speak; thirty blows, though you cannot speak." Shibayama Zenkei once registered disgust with a group of American students when they told him of an American "roshi" who, invited to give a lecture on Zen, sat in zazen posture before the audience for thirty minutes and said nothing.

Suzuki Daisetz (1870–1956), the Japanese scholar and teacher, first introduced Zen to many Western readers. Spirited, compassionate, at home in New York as well as in Kyoto and Tokyo, he opened up the vistas of Zen Buddhism through his writing and teaching. Suzuki has had his critics—especially those in Japan who have spoken against his "westernizing" tendencies and his failure to emphasize practice. He was, for me, a compelling and influential first teacher. An older colleague of mine was more fortunate; he had a "seminar" with Suzuki at Union Theological Seminary. Among many remembrances, my

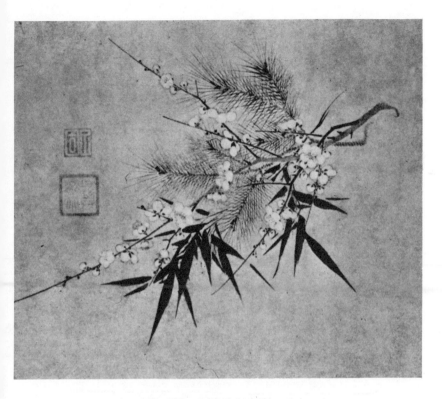

Chao Meng-chien's painting,
"The Three Friends of Cold Winter."
Plum, pine, bamboo—different things can go together.

Courtesy of National Palace Museum, Taipei.

friend recalls his Japanese teacher's refusal to engage in extensive argument and elaboration. Once my colleague asked Suzuki if he would answer some questions about the nature of Zen "emptiness." Suzuki replied, "Ahh, let's have a cup of tea." And yet he could, and did, write voluminously about Zen. In a slight paraphrase of a Suzuki definition, Zen in its essence is the art of seeing into the nature of one's being and the pointer of the way from bondage to freedom.[4]

Def.

All those who attempt to describe Zen stress its power of liberation—its concern with setting people free from their illusions and ensnarements. Hubert Benoit, a French psychoanalyst who finds Zen Buddhist insights important in his professional practice, speaks to this point. A person is frequently "caught in the entanglements of his mental representations. Everything happens as though a screen were woven between himself and reality."[5] Zen practitioners speak of the "sword of life"—that which enables a person to cut through irrelevancies, veneers, and the insincerities of relations with others.

Most Zen masters, as well as Zen poets and artists, do not present their teachings as a sect of Buddhism. Dogen, the influential thirteenth-century Japanese master, wrote, "Anybody who would regard Zen as a school or sect of Buddhism, and call it Zenshu, Zen school, is a devil."[6] Zen's primary teaching of emancipation is not thought to be represented exclusively by any one group of Zen Buddhists. Zen does not even claim that its understanding of the human situation is supreme or necessarily all-sufficient. It can be "placed alongside" other religions and perspectives. Whatever spiritual values Zen possesses are available to people of all cultures and persuasions.

Zen Buddhism traces its lineage to the historical Buddha, the "illumined one," or, as he was known during

his life, Shakyamuni, the Indian sage and teacher of the
mid sixth century B.C. Zen embraces the classical fourfold
truth and eightfold path of the Buddha,[7] but places even a
greater emphasis on certain qualities of life which the historic Buddha is thought to have displayed. Zen teachers,
along with those from other Buddhist groups, frequently
refer to the Buddha as "Tathagata," "the one who has thus
gone" or "the one who has fully come through." Buddha is
not represented by Zen as the one who gave scriptures of
divine status through his own words or through the writings of disciples. Indeed, it is typical of Zen practitioners
to question the worth of any such doctrinal assertions.
Buddha, according to Zen, warned his followers of the
confusing maze of dogma which often confronts anyone
attempting to practice a religion. One must stay away from
all needless speculation; or else, as Takeuchi Yoshinori
relates in a familiar Buddhist story, a person's curiosity and
argument will resemble the foolish deed of a man who was
hit with a poison arrow. "When his friends and kinsmen
brought a doctor to him he said, 'I will not have the arrow
drawn out until I know the man who pierced me, whether
he is a noble or brahman, a merchant or laborer. . . . What
is his name, and to which clan does he belong? . . . I will
not have the arrow drawn out until I know the type of bow
with which I was pierced, whether it is a spring-bow or a
crossbow.' "

Silent acceptance of a discipline, a serenity, and a deep
integrity are, for Zen people, the crucial marks of the
founder. "Once Buddha was together with his disciples.
He picked up a lotus flower, and as he looked at it, a smile
played upon his lips. No disciple was able to understand
his meaning. Only Kashyapa [a close disciple] smiled with
him. Buddha recognized this and said to him, 'From now
on you shall keep the heart of Buddhism.' His smile and

his silence are the same."[8] The essential relationship between the Buddha and his disciples is frequently pictured as nonverbal and hence the Buddha's teaching is known among Zen practitioners as "the wordless doctrine." Or, as a saying puts it, Buddha "with Mind transmitted Mind."

Various Indian patriarchs continued to transmit the wordless doctrine. After many generations of teaching, one patriarch left his native India, presumably in the early sixth century A.D., to teach in China. He became known as the first Chinese patriarch—the half-legendary, half-historical Bodhidharma, who allegedly confronted the Chinese emperor, crossed the Yangtze River on a reed, and spent nine years facing a wall in meditation. The Chinese Buddhist movement attributed to Bodhidharma became known as Ch'an, whose Chinese characters mean concentration or meditation. In Japanese, the characters for Zen came to have the same basic meaning. Chinese Ch'an and the later Japanese Zen became an identifiable East Asian branch of Mahayana, the northern division of Buddhism, in contrast to Hinayana or Theravada, the southern division. Ch'an endured waves of persecution in the Middle Ages in China; by the time of the Sung dynasty (960–1279 [1126]), it was the primary representative of Buddhism in China.

A short succession of patriarchs followed upon the death of Bodhidharma in China, concluding with the sixth and last, known as Eno, or Hui-neng (Wei-lang) in Chinese, who flourished around 700. No other patriarchs have been recognized by Ch'an or Zen groups in China or Japan. Bewitchingly ahistorical and anti-institutional, Ch'an stressed small communities of teachers and followers, often following different "ways." It did not insist on unified development, nor did it establish lavish temple organizations. The continuation of a patriarchate appeared to be at variance with the unfolding spirit, as well as the original conception of the movement.

Bodhidharma, who was to become known as Daruma in Japan, allegedly left behind a few short treatises and sermons. He did not try to connect Ch'an to the words or sermons of the historical Buddha; rather, Buddha was appealed to as a type, a model, even as a "way" of knowledge which all people should have before them. Bodhidharma taught that the name *Buddha* was originally a Sanskrit word meaning "initiate." The true follower of the Buddha should begin simply where she is and search within to discover her own "treasure of the heart." Buddha is not to be found outside one's own nature. The most elaborate and even the most devoted prayers, fastings, sutra readings, and observance of monastic rules will not lead one closer to a knowledge of the self or the meaning of the world. The major contribution of Bodhidharma, the succeeding Chinese patriarchs, and other early teachers was to stress the necessity of "looking within." The Ch'an teaching exemplified an ancient Chinese proverb: "The treasures of the house do not come in through the gate."

The patriarchs and subsequent Ch'an teachers were influenced greatly by existing religious traditions in China. More than Confucianism, the ancient philosophy of "the Way," or Taoism, left its mark on Ch'an. Taoism was attractive to many forms of Buddhism during the latter's entrance into China approximately at the beginning of the second century A.D. The early Ch'an teachers during the period A.D. 500 to A.D. 800 found the intuitive, nonverbal, and antidogmatic qualities of Taoism to be significant. Taoism had for some time been in quiet revolt against Confucianism; the early Taoist teachers had stressed that a practitioner could go directly to the Tao, the Way, without having to master the Confucian sayings or classics and without having to be governed by the *li,* the Confucian rites and ceremony. This implicit directness was welcomed by Ch'an leaders. Important Taoist terms were used by Ch'an and other Buddhist teachers to a wide extent. *Tao* became the established Chinese rendition for the Buddhist word *dharma,* meaning teaching or even the wider concept of reality. Sometimes *Tao* was even used to translate the word *bodhi,* or enlightenment.

Taoist teachings, along with those of Confucius, had arisen in the "central period" of Chinese history, 500 to 221 B.C.—sometimes known as the "spring" and "autumn" of Chinese history. It was the time of religious and literary renaissance which historians, and also Mao Tse-tung, have described as the "blooming of one hundred flowers." Early philosophical Taoism is based upon a short classic of some five thousand characters, the *Tao Te Ching (The Way and Its Power),* presumably written, or at least suggested in oral form, by the traditional founder Lao-tzu sometime in the sixth or fifth century B.C.

The primary concept of early philosophical Taoism and the *Tao Te Ching* for Ch'an and later Zen Buddhism was the idea of Tao itself. Chapter twenty-one of the *Tao Te Ching* reads, in part:

> The Tao is elusive and intangible.
> It is intangible and elusive, and yet within
>   is image.
> It is elusive and intangible, and yet within
>   is form.
> It is dim and dark, and yet within is essence.
> This essence is very real.

No one can say what the precise nature of the Tao is, but certainly it is a reality which has been described by Taoist,

Ch'an, and Zen writings as all-pervading, all-embracing, and in all things. In the poem it is primarily the ultimate principle of balance and harmony. The Tao is not thought to be static, however—indeed, water symbolism is most often used to explain its nature. The universal Tao, like water, seeks its own consistent level; as water covers over and wears away rocks, the Tao is perceived as spreading and smoothing over. The Tao is like running water which cannot be caught in a bucket; it will always fill to the brim and overflow in order to continue on its way. Standing as a term for unified reality, the Tao bespeaks a mystical "holism." It affords what might be called today a "gestalt" perspective. The Tao is a supreme gestalt, or universal field of reality, in which all conceivable parts are connected and interrelated. Any factionalism or separate categorization moves against the spirit and meaning of the term.

The *Tao Te Ching* also speaks of an individual tao, or the "way" of each person. An individual is to find his own balance and harmony amid the changes of the ever-flowing stream of his life. Most important, in a search for stability and tranquillity, one must continually relate one's self to the universal Tao. Gary Snyder, the American Zen poet, puts it this way: "You might say you have the sea and the waves; that one starts off by being a wave and feeling that one's almost a separate entity as a wave, and then going from that to feel that though one's still a wave, one's essentially, more importantly, part of the ocean." [9] The early Taoists would agree with Willa Cather's words, "That is happiness: To be dissolved into something great and complete." [10]

A second major contribution to Zen from the *Tao Te Ching* and early Taoism is the meaning and significance of nature. Taoist poets and landscape artists remind us that the Way can be understood as nature, or that at least nature can be conceived as a teacher of the great Tao. Nature has its own interdependencies—its ebb and flow, its warmth and cold, its tides, its seasons—and it seeks its own balance and harmony. People are part of the vast interconnections in nature. We learn about ourselves as we immerse ourselves in the natural world, sensing out association with air, water, sunlight, trees, animals. In fact, human existence *is* nature, but nature which is conscious of itself and aware of totality. Taoism also bequeathed to Zen Buddhism a sense of esthetics about the natural world. Nature's beauty calls forth human response and reverence—even though people may not fully understand nature's teaching power about the Way. Certain aspects of the natural world, because of their singular beauty, their uniqueness, are even identified with the Buddha. A saying attributed to Dogen, the influential thirteenth-century master, is: "The color of the mountains is Buddha's body; the sound of running water is his great speech." Or a Zen person might simply say, "Buddha is the twinkling of the stars."

o Ch'an and Zen are indebted to Taoism in a third fashion. The *Tao Te Ching* and the later *Chuang-tzu* speak of a way of performing or functioning known as "doing without doing," or *wei wu wei*. According to Lao-tzu, the good ruler is one who rules by not ruling; effectiveness and wisdom are manifest, and yet there is no overassertion. The *Tao Te Ching's* advice is not to overplan, not to overconcentrate, but rather to let an action and a function develop and take place. Zen picks up this stress in many instances; the physical art of judo means, in its original characters, "the gentle way." The accomplished judo athlete is not one who uses strong-arm techniques or overpowering force; rather, she converts, in a flowing way, forces that suddenly seem to be against her into leverage and power in her favor. The Japanese poet Kikaku (1660–1707), a poet of Basho's school, writes of *wei wu wei* in a famous haiku:

> The tree frog
> Riding on a banana leaf
> Trembling.[11]

A small frog is sitting on a banana leaf. The leaf bends and bends under the weight of the creature and finally bends so far that the frog slides off into the water; the leaf is left trembling. The whole action is one of continuous motion, unplanned sequence, and natural resolution. It happens by not happening. It is also an action unaccompanied by yearning for rewards or the fruits of action. Doing without doing is the spirit, a Taoist-Zen person would say, that produces great works of art, allows good lovemaking to happen, creates memorable conversations, makes possible inspired flute playing, and allows an arrow to "fall" to the target.

Ch'an Buddhism found supporting concepts in many other forms of Chinese literature and philosophy. There are strong connections between Ch'an and Zen and the ancient *I Ching,* or *The Book of Changes,* which consists of commentary in prose and poetry on hexagrams of broken and solid lines. The *I Ching* was originally a source of archaic prophecy and divination, but it developed into much more. It became a book to which a practitioner directed a specific, personal question in a ritual setting, constructed a resulting hexagram, read a commentary, and derived an answer or a response which was to be pondered, discussed, and finally compared with a second hexagram. The proper use of the *I Ching* emphasized that one must use the hexagrams and the words to "look inside" oneself in a new and perhaps startling way because of what one had visualized and read.

Without question, Ch'an and Zen contain many parallels to Chinese yin-yang thought. The thrust of this traditional archetypal perspective was to stress balance and harmony between female (yin) and male (yang), dark and light, soft and hard, northside of a mountain and southside of a mountain, earth and sky, negative and positive. In addition to harmonious relationship, it was asserted that each quality or aspect contained the seed or the germ of its opposite and would inevitably mix with and even turn into that to which it was originally opposed. Mutation and flow were thought to be indispensable parts of yin-yang stability, balance, and unity.

A more philosophical source was found in Buddhist speculative thought known as Kegon, the Japanese term for the Hua Yen school in China, dating from the T'ang period in the seventh and eighth centuries A.D. As a development of early Mahayana Buddhism, especially of the *Prajnaparamita Sutras,* the *Sutras of Transcendental Wisdom,* Kegon stressed that any particularity, especially an esthetic one, could point to and even contain the infinite. A small Zen rock-and-gravel garden portrays the simplicity and efficiency of the laws and principles governing the macrocosm. Dogen spoke in Kegon fashion about the reflection of the moon in a small area of water. "Though the light of the moon is vast and immense, it finds a home in water only a foot long and an inch wide. The whole moon and the whole sky find room enough in a single dewdrop, a single drop of water." [12] Ch'an and Zen also found most congenial the portrayal of the Buddha sitting on the lotus throne of a thousand petals, known as the Kegon, or flower wreath, in which all entities are perceived as connected and capable of entwining and entering into each other. The image of the figure seated on the interwoven wreath conveys the possibility that each particular is in communion with the Buddha and, through him, with all other things.

When Ch'an Buddhism came to Japan in the late twelfth century, it confronted Shinto, the ancient folk cult of the islands. Shinto was and is the "mother religion" of Japan, welcoming and incorporating Buddhist, Confucian, and Taoist teachings while influencing and molding them subtly into unmistakable Japanese form. Shinto cast its spell over Zen in at least two ways, helping to make the Zen of Japan different from the Ch'an of China. The contributions dealt primarily with the perceiving and experiencing of natural objects. Shinto asserted that each entity, or at least each class of objects animate or inanimate, had its own *kami,* its unique spirit, or *musubi,* life-force. A *kami* for a Shintoist is not so much a deity as it is an indication of identity and uniqueness and, beyond that, a call to mystery and wonder about the essence of a thing. The *kami* of an object is, as Shinto people are fond of saying, "caught, but not taught." Japanese Zen followers have maintained the Shinto esteem for the particularity and life-force of individual things. A certain kind of tea is not only to be savored, but also reverenced; likewise, in Zen one is urged to catch the specialness and mystery of cherry wood, a single flower, a piece of bamboo, a stone.

Second, Shinto urged upon Zen a communion with nature by sensory contact with specific things. The Taoist sense of a general immersion in nature became sharpened. The *musubi* of all objects had to be felt, smelled, touched, seen, heard. The famous ancient Shinto shrine of Ise impresses this point upon all visitors or pilgrims. As one account reads: "The visitor's contact with the Ise Shrine begins with the sound of his feet on the pebbles covering the approaches. . . . The crunching of the pebbles actually heightens the impression of stillness all about him; eventually, drawn into the monotonous repetition of the sound he produces, he forgets all conversation, and his mind is possessed by thoughts that no speech can express. A little further on, another sound begins to obliterate the sound of the pebbles: the rippling murmur of the Isuzu where it draws close to the road. At this spot known as Mitarashi, with the murmur of the water all about him, he dips his hands in the stream as a token of physical purification and in so doing is brought into still closer communion with nature." [13]

Basho (1644–94), the master of Zen haiku, often expressed these Shinto influences. In his *Narrow Road to the Deep North and Other Travel Sketches,* he writes:

> To talk casually
> About an iris flower
> Is one of the pleasures
> Of the wandering journey . . . .
> Hot radish
> Pierced my tongue,
> While the autumn wind
> Pierced my heart . . . .
> On a cool autumn day,
> Let us peel with our hands
> Cucumbers and mad-apples
> For our simple dinner

The ultimate task of the poet is to search for the *kami* of that which she writes about. Basho counsels: "Go to the pine if you want to learn about the pine, or to the bamboo if you want to learn about the bamboo . . . . Your poetry issues of its own accord when you . . . have plunged deep enough into the object to see something like a hidden glimmering there." [14]

So Zen Buddhism, like all religions, has a history of coming from and being influenced by other religions, as seen in its migration over the centuries from India through China to Japan. Nearly all practitioners of other East Asian religions can find Zen practices or points of view to be amiable and similar to their own. A Confucian, for example, would find that Zen "everydayness" is not dissimilar to his own conception of the teachings of the sage on the useful and honorable "way." Influences and parallels are ever present in the history of Zen. Does this mean that Zen is a collective of teachings drawn principally from other Buddhist, Taoist, and Shinto ideas? The answer, in part, is affirmative. Zen shares parallel insights with other traditions as they all attempt to answer the meaning of *prajna,* or wisdom. Zen ideas and perspectives are certainly not unlike those offered in ancient Hindu and Vedic sources. But the answer is also negative. Although Zen has membership in a large family of Asian religions where influence and counterinfluence abound, a combination of previous traditions in a new setting produced a singularity, as seen, principally, in Zen understandings of discipline, meditation, and esthetics.

The first major teacher of Zen in Japan was Eisai (1141–1215), who, in founding the Rinzai sect, stressed the discipline of wrestling with a koan, or the working through, during meditation, of a puzzling and jolting question. Eisai became skilled in the Ch'an use of koan during two extensive visits to Chinese retreats. During his administration of Kennin-ji in Kyoto, he refined the Ch'an Koan technique. Eisai also brought tea seeds from China, planting them in temple grounds, and helped to make tea an integral part of Zen and Japanese culture. Dogen

(1200–1253), probably the leading spirit of Japanese Zen and founder of the Soto sect, stressed the pure art of za-zen, or sitting. He was not opposed to koan; indeed, he is alleged to have spent the last night of his five-year stay in China copying part of the *Hekiganroku,* the *Blue Cliff Record,* a collection of koan "cases" and commentary. Dogen returned to Japan and became the leader of several Zen communities in cities, as well as in mountain retreats and the countryside. His treatises on zazen are unique in their directness and encouragement—written for all practition-ers, they are remarkable for their brevity (one contains less than a thousand Chinese characters) and for their human-ness.

Through the work of Eisai and Dogen and their im-mediate successors, a simplified, direct, and manageable array of concepts and practices emerged. Although similar in content and in discipline with many East Asian religious traditions, and directly dependent on the parent move-ment of Chinese Ch'an, the form and structure of Zen in Japan in the Middle Ages became identifiable.

Empty, yet full

What are the major particulars of Japanese Zen? Ruth Fuller Sasaki writes of a "direct understanding of THIS." [15] Study and work with a teacher or a master in a community over a considerable period of time are required so that one may come to know the *dharma,* the ultimate reality, or teaching, or THIS, which, according to Zen, Buddha be-queathed to his disciple Kashyapa. And Kashyapa passed the teaching in turn to others. Nishida Kitaro speaks of THIS as a "place" (*basho*). the true Zen place possesses the first wisdom of Buddha-nature, which is often called "the wisdom of the great round mirror." A mirror reflects everything, or, in an extended sense, "takes in everything." A mirror can be understood as that place where everything is included and nothing is excluded.

The substance of a mirror is its clear emptiness. The mirror in Zen is the provocative symbol for the Buddhist doctrine of *sunyata,* voidness or emptiness. To search after *dharma,* or THIS, or ultimate reality, a Zen person must stop his ego-building exercises of doing and contriving; he must become like a mirror, blank and clear, ready to reflect and take in all things. A person aspiring to the Zen place must allow that which is subjective as well as that which is objective to be reflected and taken in. Japanese Zen displays its rigor when it speaks of absolute nothingness as being a characterization of the true place of THIS. "One day a monk said to Zen master Joshu: 'I have cast away everything, and there is nothing at all left in my mind. What would you say to that?' To this Joshu gave the unexpected reply, 'Cast *that* away!' The monk insisted, 'I have told you that there is nothing left in me. What should I cast away?' Joshu then said, 'In that case, keep on carrying it.' " [16] To boast of having cast away everything is not to follow the way of absolute nothingness or to live in *sunyata.*

A sense of interconnection or "joinedness" follows as a mark of the true Zen place. The Zen life transcends the dualities of space and time, form and substance, mind and body. One is mindful of parts and lives happily in a world of segments and divisions, but one also searches for the deeper reality of connection and nonduality. The Zen master Tozan said: "The blue mountain is the father of the white cloud. The white cloud is the son of the blue mountain. All day long they depend on each other, without being dependent on each other. The white cloud is always the white cloud. The blue mountain is always the blue mountain." [17]

Cloud and mountain are separate, but they also belong together. One is always aware of their differences, but there will be times when the cloud is low lying, more gray than white, enshrouding the mountain—with only now and then a breakthrough of rock and ridge. On such a day, mountain and cloud are enmeshed and joined. Even on a clear "mountain day" when they are distinctly separate, white cloud and blue mountain are connected in one's range and focus of vision and in one's esthetic of "seeing." Their unity comes to expression in and through their difference and is sensed and confirmed by the viewer. Unity for Zen does not "lie under" difference; the concept is not assumed as a starting point or taken as a precondition, as it is in much of Indian thought. Rather, unity arises out of real difference and can only be grasped in the experience of things truly distinct.

An eighth-century Chinese poem, influential in Japanese Zen, speaks of the nonduality of space and time:

> The wild geese fly across the long sky above.
> Their image is reflected upon the chilly
>   water below.
> The geese do not mean to cast their image
>   on the water;
> Nor does the water mean to hold the image
>   of the geese.[18]

One interpretation is that the geese, flying at a fast speed across the horizon, represent time, and that the pond, in its stillness and expanse, represents space. But at one instant of reflection time is reflected in space and space "holds" time. The geese are still geese and the pond is the pond, but at one special moment they and the deeper aspects of time and space, which they symbolize, come together. The

Zen person is to use her discipline and her powers of observation to find such points of fusion.

Also, the divisions and segments of personal time, in all their reality and uniqueness, have the power of creating a unity. In response to the question, "What is the nature of my true self?" the traditional Zen answer has been, "Your original face before your parents were born." The true self is to be sought and known in the present, but it has an inseparable connection with its past and also with its future and its potential. Think of your true nature as coming out of many generations, connected with forces and impulses which are beyond your power of comprehension, *and* as having a "time ahead"—but also as revealing and producing an ongoing single process. Do not separate past, present, and future; see them as helpful distinctions, but remember that such divisions by themselves cannot account for the ultimate reality of selfhood.[19] Rather, a connection and a holism are to be sought.

Nonduality is not to be confused with oneness or union. Oneness is a concept that can be readily postulated and conceived, but nonduality and Zen unity cannot be grasped so easily. An imaginative and provoking Zen statement is that "nonduality is not one, not two, not both, and not neither." As the *Avatamsaka Sutra* of Kegon Buddhism puts it:

> In the higher real of true Suchness
> There is neither "self" nor "other":
> When direct identification is sought,
> We can only say, "not two."
>
> In being "not two" all is the same,
> All that is comprehended in it;
> The wise in the ten quarters,
> They all enter in the Absolute Reason . . . .

Infinitely small things are as large as large
    things can be,
For here no external conditions obtain;
Infinitely large things are as small
    as small things can be,
For objective limits are here of no consideration.[20]

Nonduality does not deny the discernible separateness of
self and other, small things and large things, mountain and
cloud, wise people "living in ten quarters"—distinctions
necessary for ongoing human discourse and understanding. But the Zen point of view is to stress a "higher order"
arising out of difference and the way of seeing and comprehension. The emphasis is on a vantage point where
separations and identifications remain, but also where the
differentiations are gathered up in the totality of the
dharma, or supreme reality.

There is a highly experiential note about nonduality. It
is not achieved through a series of constructs; it happens
when seeing, practice, and experience make it possible.
Although always potential, nonduality is to be sensed and
grasped in special and oft-repeated circumstances. The
Zen advice is to seize and finally make rhythmical in one's
discipline and esthetic experience such revelatory occasions. Basho imaginatively presented a moment of experiencing nonduality when he wrote a "snowstorm"
haiku:

Snow-isolated . . .
Once more I press
My back against
My thinking post.[21]

In the Zen search for THIS, that place of absolute
nothingness where joinedness and nonduality are possible,

a close association with Taoism is present once more. In describing a wheel, the *Tao Te Ching* in chapter eleven speaks of "thirty spokes joined at the hub"—a center where there is emptiness. The Zen approach goes beyond the Taoist in stressing the sense of function and activity present in the proper meaning of nothingness. We may be like beads on a string, empty in the center and "selfless," but this does not mean that we are not functioning and acting. We should be "empty, but awake," as one saying puts it. Zen emptiness can be compared with the concept of zero in mathematics and computer science. Zero itself contains nothing, yet it has the possibility of changing a statement drastically, depending on where it is placed— and on how many zeros are used. Zero is not nihilistically empty. As a Taoist-Zen phrase states, "The void is void, also, of voidness."

If one peels away the unnecessary layers of ego and "busy-ness" in order to find the true "place," one will be able to function and move in a new way with vigor and purpose. That the true self is resident in each of us is always affirmed by Zen. With similarity to Freudian psychoanalytic theories, the self does not have to be "constructed," nor does it need the help of any doctrine or outside perspective. The Zen technique of liberation allows a practitioner to cut through the inflated ego, feeding on its misconceptions, to the true self, living in and pursuing emptiness, joinedness, and nonduality.

A discipline

The seemingly intense discipline and formal structure of Zen are often difficult to understand, let alone appreciate. I recall the comments of a student who came as an invited guest to a sesshin, a concentrated retreat, where strict Zen procedures were being followed in connection with sit-

tings. He had been involved in a variety of practices connected with meditation. He said to me after the end of a
very structured day: "I can't take this any more—the bowing, the sitting 'just this way,' the clappers, the slow walking afterwards. I'm looser and freer." Paul Wienpahl tells
of a visit he made to a Japanese friend's home; he stepped
out into the garden and sat on a rock—the day was sunny
and the scene inviting: "It was a delicious experience, but
in a few moments I was informed that I should not sit out
there. The garden was designed to be viewed from the
room (thus I could not see its beauty from where I was),
and I was cluttering it up. I stepped back into the room and
looked for the beauty of the garden, but now I could not
find it."[22] Formalism and structure can become oppressive
and stifling in Zen.

Yet Zen views its discipline not as overbearing formalism or a mere set of rules, but as a means to emancipation. One engages in the discipline in order to be set free
from restraints on function and productivity. Walter
Gropius spoke a Zen phrase when he summarized his impression of the work of a Japanese architect: "Develop an
infallible technique, and then place yourself at the mercy
of inspiration."[23] So necessary and fundamental is discipline to Zen that Dogen and other masters have said simply: "Practice is enlightenment." The ongoingness of one's
practice is to be embraced. No emancipation will occur
unless there is perseverance and concentration on the particular discipline at hand. Master Ummon remarked, "If
you walk, just walk. If you sit, just sit. But don't wobble."[24]

Initial Zen advice about practice might be: Do not be
overly concerned about the purpose of your discipline.
Become engaged in it and let the significance come upon
you. Become repetitive in order that a natural rhythm

about your discipline may be established. Philip Kapleau tells of a pianist who played a puzzling and tantalizing contemporary piece before an audience. At the conclusion, a listener asked, "What does it mean?" Without a word, the pianist sat down and played it through again; after he finished the second time, he said, "That's what it means."

Rather than offering theories about sitting or mind-body training, Zen encourages its practitioners to begin. A Basho haiku reads:

> First winter rain.
> The monkey also seems to wish a tiny
> Cloak of straw.[25]

One interpretation is that the poet is referring to the insignificant beginning of one's practice in zazen—that such a beginning is simple, natural, and desirable, like the first rain of winter. Yet, beginning and continuing in a discipline protect one against the cold and all other elements which prevent, symbolically, the full discovery of one's true self.

Zen speaks of four major forms of discipline: zazen or meditation, the wrestling with a koan or mondo, participation in some form of body discipline or awareness, and esthetic appreciation.

Zazen and chanting

Typically, a Zen master will begin a discussion of zazen by describing how it is done. A practitioner assumes a position which will be some variant of a "lotus posture." She may sit in the full-lotus position, with the soles of each foot facing upward on top of each crossed knee, possibly each thigh; she may sit in a half-lotus position, with only one foot tucked up; or she may sit "Burmese style" with her legs folded, but feet and ankles on the floor. Or it may suit a practitioner's body structure and comfort to sit "Japanese style," with legs folded directly to the rear and buttocks nearly resting on the heels. Firm pillows or folded blankets are used for support in each position. While there is a strong preference for a lotus position, in the end a person must choose that posture which is most solid for her and allows the greatest powers of concentration. Whatever posture she chooses, it is important to keep the back straight, the knees in contact with the floor, the hands folded on the lap with the left hand resting loosely on top of the right and the thumbs touching at the tips. The head should be held erect, continuing the straightness of the spine, and the eyes should be half open, sighting downward at some spot approximately a foot and a half in front of the knees.

The sitting position should be one in which a feeling of ongoing stability can be sensed. Masters often say, "You should sit like a great mountain." One's position, above all, should produce a feeling of serenity. It is often said, "When sitting, you are in the deep of your being."

The practice of zazen becomes the way in which one searches for the place of nothingness, the sense of interconnection or joinedness, and the grasping of nonduality. It becomes such a practice when one has the feeling of being "confined to an ice cave ten thousand miles thick." [26] Zazen becomes the occasion when one employs the ego in a conscious decision to meditate but gradually wears it out like a pair of shoes as the practice continues. [27]

Like many Hindu and Buddhist disciplines, zazen stresses a concentration on breathing. Inhaling through the nose by expanding the diaphragm (not by raising the chest), you take a normal full, slow breath. A Zen teacher will stress that during inhalations it should seem as if the air is coming to you, not that you are forcing or drawing it in. And likewise during exhalations, air is simply leaving, not being ejected. To concentrate more fully on the natural process of breathing, a simple counting technique is prescribed. As you exhale, slowly count one, trying to take the number one and place it in your abdomen, or in your *hara* region, the space considered to be four fingers' width below the navel and the area which contains vital organs and constitutes "mid-body." Counting exhalations should continue to ten and then begin over again. When you are more experienced, inhalations may be counted. In all instances of simple breathing concentration, you are trying to transfer consciousness or awareness to the midsection, away from the brain and cerebral processes.

You are urged to conceive of inhalations as coming from "the center of the world." You give your breath back to the world. Think of two short wooden clapper sticks used at the beginning of zazen; consider one standing vertically on the other forming an upside-down *T*; the vertical stick represents arms, chest, and head, and the horizontal hips and legs. Picture the clappers so arranged on top of a large bronze circle or gong: You conceive of breath as coming to you from the center of the circle or disk beneath you, symbolizing the world, and you give breath back to the same source.

The length of the sitting varies greatly with occasion and experience of one's practice. During a sesshin, or retreat and period of great concentration, individual sittings may last fifty minutes or more. More often, especially for beginners, sittings run twenty minutes each. Upon arising from a sitting, members place their palms together and bow to each other in an expression of gassho, or gratitude. They may also bow to their individual sitting places, both at the beginning and at the end of a zazen period. Between sittings mediators engage in kinhin, or walking zazen. After bowing to each other, the hands are placed together over the *hara* region on the abdomen, thumbs interlocked, right hand facing in, left hand covering. A slow walking around the perimeter of the room in a continuous flowing motion is begun. At a signal, the pace of the kinhin is increased. Members of the sitting then stop and form a circle or oval and bow once more in expression of gratitude to each other. Kinhin and gassho are done at the end of the last sitting of the practice as well as between sittings.

Most periods of zazen, particulary those which are part of a daily discipline or service or held during a sesshin, are accompanied by chanting. Parts of the *Prajnaparamita Sutras,* especially the *Diamond Sutra* and the *Heart Sutra,* will be chanted, accompanied by drum, gong, and stick clapping. Participants commit to memory in Japanese (reading at first, if they are Westerners, from a chanting book containing syllabized Japanese) large sections of sutras, as well as other classical statements. A typical chant as part of zazen, introducing other parts of the sitting, is the "Kaikyoge," "On Opening the Sutra":

> The Dharma, incomparably profound and
>   minutely subtle,
> Is hardly met with, even in hundreds of thousands
>   of millions of eons,
> We now can see it, listen to it, accept
>   and hold it·
> May we completely understand the Tathagata's
>   true meaning [28]

The exact procedure of sitting, gassho, kinhin, hand posture, and chanting vary in different temples and centers. Soto Zen people most often do zazen facing the wall; Rinzai people face each other. There is, however, surprising harmony in all forms of Zen practice. I prefer to sit facing others, spread around the perimeter of a room, mixed male and female. It does not take a major adjustment, however, to sit in the New York zendo, or hall, presided over by Shimano-roshi, where participants face the wall for most sittings, males on one side and females on the other.

Not only is the discipline basically the same, but so are the problems—whether in Kyoto, New York, Rochester, California, or Williamstown, and whether Rinzai or Soto. The practitioner fights sleepiness (even sometimes when she seems most refreshed); a limb goes to sleep; a straight back on a particular day is hard to maintain; and breathing is not relaxed. A mediator has the feeling that she must somehow "break through" to proper concentration. Because of its belief in the importance of the physical and in the power of the abrupt, Zen practice often employs a kyosaku, or special flat-bladed stick, to arouse and redirect the energy of the sitters. The sitting master or assistant will deliver, upon request, two sharp blows on the shoulder muscles close to the neck on each side. Sometimes, as a substitute, firm hand slaps are delivered to the upper middle of the back between the shoulder blades while the practitioner bends forward with head on the floor and back parallel to the floor. The effect of these blows, never mandatory, produces a sudden awareness and awakening of body; a stimulation to sitting posture; a loosening of back or shoulder muscles; and, most important, a sense of crossing a boundary, marked by sound and feeling, into a new realm of concentration and relaxation. The sitter feels that her problems have been confronted in a new way and that centering has now a better chance.

But problems still remain—even for the most experienced practitioners. Before and after the kyosaku, thoughts will arise during zazen connected with the day's routine ("After sitting, I'll do errands, then I'll go to the library . . . "); fantasies will predominate; and dreams will return. "Do not fight them," is the advice of Zen masters about such distractions. Bankei-roshi said that contesting against thoughts is "like washing off blood with blood." [29] Rather, the sitter should identify such thoughts, so prevalent at the beginning of a sitting, and "invite them into himself"—but then let them go. Bassui writes, "Do not try to prevent thoughts from arising and do not cling to any that have arisen." [30] A practitioner recognizes that distractions will arise, allows them to come, but also lets them pass through him to a place apart as he continues on the way toward concentration and centering.

The practice of zazen is considered by most masters and adherents to be a rhythmic, ordinary part of one's total functioning. The practice is not motivated by any desire to achieve, but rather by the hope of "seeing" the truth about one's existence and the world. One should not use zazen as a means or instrument in some personal progress scheme, or engage in it to be totally different than one was before. These aims are all connected with *dukkha,* or the suffering or conflict which come from desire. Such manipulated uses of meditation produce dividedness rather than integration. Nor is zazen an escape from the world; it is rather a way of reentering the world in a new way. As Yung-chia wrote:

> The man who clings
> to vacancy
> neglecting the world
> of things
> escapes from drowning
> but leaps into the fire.[31]

Above all, the practitioner does not glorify or feel herself to be exalted above others. She does not play the game of "Zenner than thou." Over and again, the central practice is asserted to be "nothing special, nothing special."

For me, once again, the remarkably simple statue of Ganjin, the Chinese monk who came to Japan in the mid-eighth century and spent the rest of his life founding a center in Nara, is symbolic. He sits erect, but not tight. He sits composed and integrated. The artist has caught the power of Ganjin's centering and concentration. He appears ready, upon completion of his sitting, to rise and return to his teaching or to his manual work. The statue impresses the viewer as simple, "nothing special," but possessing direction and stability.

2. Koan and mondo

A second distinguishing characteristic of Zen discipline is the use of koan or mondo. These are sudden, jarring statements put to a Zen practitioner by a teacher or master; their purpose is to break down artificial reasoning and categorization so that one may see more "directly." Koan and mondo discipline are more important for the Rinzai than for the Soto sect of Japanese Zen. However, Soto masters will, from time to time, break away from concentration on zazen in order to offer practitioners the complementary path of self-discovery found in koan work.

The tradition of using sharp, probing questions, to be puzzled over and wrested with for weeks, even months, is a practice deeply embedded in the history of Ch'an Buddhism. Toward the end of the southern Sung dynasty in the early thirteenth century, koan studies were established to correct the stagnation of Zen in the northern Sung dynasty, in the hopes of recapturing the vitality of Ch'an known in the T'ang dynasty (618–906). The *Mumonkan,* the *Gateless*

Gate, published in China toward the end of the southern Sung dynasty is a typical robust koan collection.

It is useful—or at least it has been in my practice and teaching of Zen—to make a distinction between koan and mondo. The characters for koan convey the meaning "catechism" or a "public proposal." A koan will usually begin with a question put to a student, followed by the seemingly nonsensical reply of the master. Here is a brief, typical example: "A monk asked master Tozan, 'What is Buddha?' Tozan said, 'Three pounds of flax.'" Usually a particular set of questions and answers are accorded near-canonic status, such as the forty-eight koans in the *Mumonkan* or those in the *Hekiganroku,* the *Blue Cliff Record.* Work on such classic statements during zazen and in discussion with one's master is designed to lead the participant away from dependence on speculative thought and a belief in the separation of subject and object. Such exercises, stressing a "break away" from ordinary analysis and conception, are often slow to have their effect upon a practitioner.

A mondo, whose characters mean a "saying," more literally "mouth in the gate," is most often a statement about aspects of nature, tending to stress emptiness and unity. One mondo, prepared by students on a cold, January, powder-snow evening (modeled on an ancient Zen saying), is "Pick up snow and the moon sparkles in your hand." A mondo will often point to the wholeness and interconnectedness of nature. Mondo represents in Japanese Zen the Shinto meaning of *kensho,* stressing the art of seeing into the beauty and wholeness of natural things. Mondo also represents the haiku tradition in Japanese literature, which moves from the observed microcosm in nature to the unity symbolized by the thing observed. If a person does catch the sparkle of the moon in the dry snowflakes in her hand, she is reminded of the closeness and relatedness of sky and earth and of the particular revelatory power of a moment of beauty. I have found it more meaningful for Western students to begin with a mondo saying in the haiku, naturalist tradition than to begin with an enigmatic, catechetical koan.

Both koan and mondo are used to bring practitioners closer to the power and meaning of zazen so that they may come to sense the "place" of emptiness, interconnection, and nonduality.

3 *Use of the body*

Gary Snyder reports that his teacher Oda-roshi once told him, "Zen is two things: meditation and sweeping the garden. . . ." [32] Many things come to mind in the phrase "sweeping the garden." One is a reference to the compassionate strain in Zen, namely, taking care of the surroundings, including both people and things; but clearly another reference is to the Zen concern with the use of the body. It is important to move, to work, to make, to create, to sweat, even to become tired—and in all such pursuits to be aware of one's body. Sweeping a garden, building a stone wall, aikido (the art of body movement in self-defense and ego confrontation), archery, chanting, brush-and-ink drawing, and walking are, at their simplest levels, necessary alternatives to the quiet concentration of zazen. Not only do such physical activities provide a natural change from meditation, but they make it possible for a practitioner to reenter zazen in a more meaningful way. In the middle of a long period of sitting and chanting in the New York zendo, the participants will suddenly lean forward and shout with full voice the Japanese word *Mu,* meaning "No" or "Not possible" or "Nothing." The word is the traditional answer given to a famous koan, "Has a dog the

Buddha nature or not?" For those working on the koan and for those not, the volume, the reverberation in mouth and throat, the intensity of the shout and the physicalness of the moment are similar to the sense of redirection given by the kyosaku, or stick. After the startling *"Mu,"* the leader of the sitting then says abruptly, "Zazen," and one is ready to pursue centeredness with new concentration and evenness.

But physical activity has a greater meaning in Zen than needed alternation and redirection. The physical affords a way to move toward that which is proclaimed in zazen and koan study. The *dharma* "place" of nothingness, the sense of interconnection, and the meaning of nonduality can be understood and sensed in the unified movements of archery, or the proper brush-and-ink drawing of bamboo leaves and shoots. The participant in a Zen physical, manual, or artistic activity is to develop certain powers of intuition and function. In brush-and-ink drawing, known as *sumi-e,* the painter, even though a beginner, must have the whole idea of the painting in mind; the drawing should be done quickly without retouching; and a technique should be developed so that arm, brush, mind, ink stone, and fingers all seem one. As *sumi-e* teachers say, one should be so undivided, coordinated, and spontaneous that "the brush draws itself." The stress on interconnection and coordination is made over and again in Zen physical pursuits. Not only must the parts of the body work together, so that one refuses to make a distinction between left and right sides, between upper and lower parts, or between windup and follow-through, but also the parts of the skill or craft must not be segmented. The Zen master of archery teaches his pupils to feel the stretching of the bow, the momentary pause at full extension, and the release as one, being conceived and accomplished without division or separate "intention."

The proper use of the body as a discipline in Zen demonstrates, in large part, its inheritance from Taoism. The student of Zen archery or of aikido, for example, is urged to be so unselfconsciously and naturally involved in her pursuit that she accords with the Taoist virtue of *wei wu wei,* "doing without doing." Moreover, true physical activity is understood in connection with a Taoist assumption that there is a flow of energy in the universe. The great Tao, or Way, is not static but conceived to be in subtle, powerful motion like the ocean in its tidal ebb and flow. Force and movement are at large in the world. The student is urged to join this cosmic energy flow and to meld her particular activity with it. To discover this "life energy," or *ki,* and to have it function in the body is what aikido stresses. The person who joins her physical activity with the *ki* is moving away from ego and developing "no mind" about herself and her activities.

A Zen swordsman so joins his efforts with the cosmic energy that he can avoid the error of "stopping"—*suki*—in the delivery of his blows (now done with padded staves) and in his footwork. The true swordsman does not let his eye fasten on, or his motion stop with, the moves of his partner. He follows through in his actions, responding where he must to his partner's moves, but not hesitating or becoming attached to what seems an obstacle. He tries to let *ki* flow through him smoothly and effectively. This understanding of universal energy properly taken inside the self is what a Zen archery master has in mind when he says, "The shot falls to the target."

Lastly, the use of the body in a physical discipline or in manual work or in an esthetic pursuit is important in Zen because of the general Buddhist stress on a knowledge of the surrounding world. One should see the world in all of

its details, those that produce suffering and those that produce joy. The confrontation with the world cannot be
done cerebrally or at a distance. Trungpa Chogyam, a
Tibetan Buddhist, puts the matter this way: "Some work
and physical effort are necessary. If we go somewhere on
foot, we know that way perfectly, whereas if we go by
motor car or airplane we are hardly there at all; it becomes
a dream. Similarly, in order to see the continual pattern of
development we have to go through it manually. That is
one of the most important things of all. And here discipline becomes necessary." [33]

I never met Suzuki Shunryu, the former spiritual director of Zen Center in San Francisco and Tassajara, a Zen
community in the heart of the California coastal mountains
south of Monterey. But I have often talked with his students; I have read his words in *Wind Bell;* and I have taught
and read many times his *Zen Mind, Beginner's Mind.* Along
with Shimano Eido of the New York Zendo and Abe
Masao in Kyoto, I count Suzuki-roshi as an influential
teacher for me in the Zen way. His death in December
1971 has not diminished his being a presence to me—as is
the case with a host of other Americans. Suzuki-roshi not
only led others in zazen, founded a genuine Zen community, offered encouragement, and practiced compassion,
but he knew and taught about the meaning and use of the
body. He was not known as an aikido expert, nor would
any of his close associates necessarily say that he was an
athlete, but he did love to work in the Tassajara garden; he
spent hours building stone walls and making rock-and-
crushed-stone "dry gardens." Those who watched him and
worked beside him in these pursuits saw him become re-
newed for zazen and other activities—and became re-
newed themselves. They saw all parts of his body coordi-
nate as he selected, picked up, moved, and aligned stones;

they were conscious of an energy flowing through Suzuki-roshi to that which was being created; they beheld him working effortlessly, even at the very end of his last illness; and they were aware of his practicing "no mind" in his physical concentration.

Esthetics

A person of the Zen way is concerned with and sensitive toward the beautiful. To live in esthetic awareness is hardly a structured discipline and practice like zazen; it is rather an intuitive attitude to be discovered and nurtured within oneself. Just as a Zen person does not have to be an athlete, or even interested in formal athletics, in order to know the proper use of the body, so a person does not have to be an artist or even skilled in the history and forms of the visual arts in order to appreciate and enter into the world of the beautiful. What is required is that one appreciate a certain kind of beauty.

Zen beauty is inescapably connected with simplicity, subtlety, and naturalness. That which is ornamented, too direct, and too declarative would not be thought of as esthetic, no matter how fascinating such an object might be technically or historically. Chojiro, a sixteenth-century potter and tea master, created a much admired tea bowl—so striking in the Zen sense that it was given the name *Shobu,* or "The Flower." The bowl is *raku* ware of gray and black, with touches of coral; it is in between the "summer" and the "winter" size. As one views this delicate bowl from different sides, or, if fortunate enough, holds it and turns it, one is strongly attracted to the subtlety of colors and the shape. But there is no flower painted on it; nor is a stalk, a leaf, a bloom even hinted at in the lines. But, suddenly, as one takes in the combination of plainness and artistry, the whole bowl becomes the flower. Out of simplicity and indirectness, comes an overwhelming esthetic statement.

The power of haiku poetry to capture the beauty and meaning of a particular moment is dependent upon similar qualities. Basho said about his art: "The haiku that reveals seventy to eighty percent of its subject is good. Those that reveal fifty to sixty percent we never tire of."[34] Beauty never reveals itself, according to Zen, in large doses; the Grand Canyon would be appreciated, but there would be greater exultation over the shimmering colors of a spring freshet as it cuts through a meadow. Yamada Hisashi, director of the Tea Ceremony Society of Urasenke in New York City, has a *kakemono,* or hanging scroll, which he often places on the walls of his tea room. Its three characters read *hana sho sho,* "flowers here and there." An interpretation of the expression is that beauty is found simply and in small clusters. It is not found, according to Zen, along groomed paths between large beds of nodding irises or waving daffodils. It is more likely to be found in a special rock, resting "just so" in the middle of a dry garden. The sense of something sparse and unadorned, "being as it ought to be"—that which is an attribute of the Tathagata or the Buddha himself—is found hither and yon and, hence, potentially everywhere. Such beauty often appears singly and in a form easily overlooked.

Zen and Ch'an art is always concerned with the balance between simple lines in brush marks and blank space. Natural objects like mountains, trees, streams, and waterfalls are never piled up on one another as they often are in literati or Confucian painting. The lines of a Zen monochrome hint at the subject and leave much to the imagination of the viewer. The painter is urged to have in mind the Chinese word *li* which originally meant the delicate markings in jade or the grain in wood; an artist should try for minimal suggestive form. The *Diamond Sutra* and others of the *Prajnaparamita Sutras* stress over and again that "form is emptiness and emptiness is form." The lines of a painting should be sparse and thus allow blankness and emptiness to be present, rather than present a subject matter drawn in detail. Gukei Ue (fl. 1370), a Zen painter-priest who studied the Sung master Mu-ch'i, painted a landscape in which he portrayed a stooped fisherman bringing home his nets. Blankness and indistinct gray dominate the painting; the lines and dark areas are few; much of the scroll is blank; the fisherman is overshadowed by the hint of a mountain; it is not clear whether he has emerged from the water or is still wading ashore; the viewer cannot tell if his nets contain anything. The painting suggests human work and motion, frailness, transitoriness, and inescapable connection with nature—all presented in suggestive, arrested style. To portray these themes with a Zen spirit, the artist used form and lines which depend on emptiness for their effectiveness and an emptiness which is present only because of the lines and form.

Zen speaks about the attitude of the maker—and the viewer—as well as about the content and nature of the beautiful. She who writes a haiku poem about a mountain or who makes a tea bowl must have the attitude of *makoto, or sincerity*. The poet or the potter must be interested in the object being portrayed or created for its own sake; she must not be "impositional" in her few words, describing the mountain in terms of her own preconceived notions; she must not be slavish to standards of color or shape, but must let the clay speak for itself as it is being formed under her hands. To practice *makoto* means to let the object emerge naturally; it means not placing oneself in the way of allowing something to become what it is supposed to be.

The Zen person, whether artist or viewer, will be attracted to objects which have *sabi*—a quality which bespeaks incompleteness, delicacy, reducedness, age, graybrownness, indistinctness. The weather-beaten boards of an old shrine or of a barn have *sabi*. The grain and lines of the wood stand out; the color is faded; the surface is rough; and an exterior emptiness covers an inner fullness. The person who appreciates *sabi* in things is said to have a *wabi* spirit. Esthetically he is pleased with the nondramatic, the fading, the plain, with that which superficially is "poor in spirit."

Finally, concerning attitude towards the esthetic, a Zen viewer will practice the meaning of simple, unfeigned exclamation or of silence when confronting the beautiful. Words and discourse are of no avail when viewing a Zen rock-and-stone garden, or a tea house with *sabi*, or a single blossom. Teishitsu, who destroyed all of his three thousand haiku except the following and two others, speaks of this.

> I came to praise the cherry blossom. "Oh! . . ."
> That's all upon Mount Yoshino.

And so does Ryota:

> The host said not a word. The guest was dumb.
> And silent, too, the white chrysanthemum.[35]

Humor

Christmas Humphreys remarks that Zen believes in and uses "more honest 'belly laughter'" than any other religion.[36] To be jocular, to use an amusing and telling anecdote, to share infectious laughter with others, to redirect a conversation through an uproarious response, to free oneself and detach oneself through the comic, to let laughter break open a terse remark—all these are part of the Zen way. Rinzai said, "Sportively and supersensuously I enter freely into all situations and apply myself as if I were not at all engaged in anything." [37]

Other religious perspectives certainly make use of humor and play, but not to the extent or in the same way as Zen. The *Bhagavad-Gita,* for example, develops the sense of play, or *lila,* which takes place between the Lord Krishna and the devotee Arjuna; in other expressions of Krishna worship, developing *Gita* themes, sexual play and cavorting between Krishna and his chief consort Radha are often present. Krishna and all his believers engage in a "back and forth," involving deception, spontaneity, and laughter. But in Hinduism the humorous, jesting relationship occurs between humans and a god; the instances are used to portray a dimension of the grace and pervasive power of Krishna and to speak of the dependence upon the divine being which all believers should have. Zen humor is not something that passes between the human and the divine, and it is not used as a way of explaining the meaning and reception of grace.

At its simplest level, Zen humor is a way of seeing and describing things. It aims at the particular and wishes to portray and object or a situation refreshingly and "as it is." Zen humor makes a realistic observation without necessarily pronouncing a judgment; it can provide a spoof, but seldom a denunciation. Issa's little observation on marriage is to the point:

> Those two tired dolls
> In the corner
> There . . . Ah yes
> They are man and wife.[38]

In its phenomenological cast—its concern with the way things are and with what is taking place—Zen humor often is used to describe a person. It will deal with his singularity, the sharpness and edgedness of his presence, his "diamond-sutra"-like qualities, without comparing his perspectives and mode of operation with another style or declaring their superiority. Paul Wienpahl tells a story of a brash American who was being guided about a Zen temple by an abbot whose English was workable, but not precise. The abbot bowed before the many *bodhisattva* statues in the buildings of the temple. The visitor was clearly bothered by this and finally said: "I thought that you were a Zen Buddhist and free of all this bowing and scraping. Hell, *I'm* freer than you. I can spit on these statues." "Okay," said the abbot, "You spits, I bows." [39]

Zen people use the comic to demystify their teachings, to proclaim a human way of understanding, and to show that their practice is "nothing special." At an alleged meeting with a devout emperor of China, Bodhidharma was asked about the essence of the "holy Buddhist doctrine." "Majesty," replied the first patriarch, "there is no doctrine—and nothing holy about it whatever." Bodhidharma and his successors, on their travels through China, are often depicted as describing Ch'an teachings as a huge joke. The Buddha himself is often pictured in a humanized, comical way. He communicated and taught with the twinkle of an eye and the flash of a smile. Issa reminds all those who visit the impressive wooden statue of the Buddha at Nara of a certain Zen spirit:

> Out from the hollow
> Of Great Buddha's nose—
> Comes a swallow.[40]

Ikkyu almost attacks the Buddha, lest he be conceived of as having special powers to bequeath to followers:

Shakyamuni
That mischievous creature,
Having appeared in this world—
How many, many people, alas,
Have been misled by him![41]

Zen humor debunks and undercuts perceptions and even practice in order to focus on the perils of attachment and illusion. The comic spirit plays a role similar to the *Diamond Sutra*'s special logic and dialectic which wrest its readers away from dependence on categories, arrogant learning, and intellectual smugness. Few things are more criticized in Zen practice than she who is so sure that her discipline is beyond reproach or, worse yet, than she who lets it be known by word, manner, the tilt of head, the movement of eyebrow that she has achieved enlightenment. It is said that such people "stink of Zen," and that their very Zennishness is self-defeating.[42] A story is told of the Ch'an teacher Hogen, who once said to a group of monks visiting his temple: "There is a big stone. Do you consider it to be inside or outside your mind?" One of the visitors, eager, ready, and superior, immediately offered what he believed to be the correct reply from the sutras, "From the Buddhist viewpoint everything is an objectification of mind, so I would say that the stone is inside my mind." "Your head," said Hogen, "must be very heavy." [43]

Bunsei, a mid-fifteenth-century Zen monastic and painter of Kyoto, entitled one of his few exquisite drawings *The Three Laughers of Tiger Ravine*. This early important Japanese ink painting shows three well-known gentlemen, a Buddhist, a Confucian, and a Taoist, turning toward each other and breaking out in uncontrolled laughter. The Confucian and the Taoist had come to visit the Buddhist teacher Hui-yuan, an important late-fourth-century formulator of Mahayana concepts in China. Hui-yuan had joined the Tung-lin monastery on Mount Lu and founded, as an adjunct, the Hermitage of the Eastern Grove. He vowed never to leave the hermitage. While strolling with his friends at the end of the visit, enjoying last-minute conversations and saying good-bye, Hui-yuan inadvertently crossed a bridge over a small ravine which marked the boundary of the hermitage. The bridge was no sooner crossed than the three men heard the roar of a tiger; startled by the sound, they suddenly realized that Hui-yuan's vow had been broken and, facing each other, they peeled forth in wild laughter. The Zen master Bunsei drew the faces with careful detail, showing a gleeful intensity as the situation is grasped; the body postures of the three are slightly off balance, as if rocked by the impact of what has happened. In a comic response to each other they grasped a crucial meaning, namely, that the spiritual integrity of a man cannot be determined by contrived boundaries. Hui-yuan was obviously a free, enlightened man of wisdom, inside the boundary or outside.

The painting also shows the three laughing over another Zen insight. A functioning, integrated, compassionate person is not bound by any one of the three religions represented by the laughers. One must cross the boundaries of any given tradition and be somewhere else, at least for awhile—just as Hui-yuan crossed Tiger Ravine—in order to be emancipated and fully human.

> Why do they laugh?
> The clouds that make no pledges
> Pass over the mountain bridge,
> Morning or evening,
> With the utmost freedom! [44]

Bunsei's painting of
"The Three Laughters of Tiger Ravine."
A Confucian and a Taoist sage laugh with
a Buddhist monk (left) who has just broken a vow.

Courtesy of Kimiko and John Powers Collection, New York.

So Bunsei offers his viewers a brush-and-ink scene in which uproariousness and glee playfully question practice, vows, and even traditions.

Koan are often put in the form of comic riddles because humor, according to Zen, has the power of diverting the mind and forcing it to look at a situation or a problem in a different way. Work on koan during meditation should take a student into the very depth of his being, redirecting and realigning perceptions. There will be discouragement and frustration; the Great Doubt of Hakuin will arise; or the "ball of doubt," mentioned by other masters, will form. These barriers must be encountered and worked through. A traditional Zen poem reads:

> Everywhere I went I met with words,
> But I couldn't understand them.
> The ball of doubt within my heart
> Was as big as a wicker basket.

After a certain point, more words or lectures certainly will not break through the Great Doubt—nor necessarily will longer and longer periods of zazen, nor will less and less sleep, nor greater denial of food, nor more agonizing concentration. Something has to enter obliquely and shatter a slavish dependence on the discipline itself. Humor has that capability, and when its power is grasped, the great ball of doubt becomes a resilient ball of play bouncing back from the cold wall of a practitioner's logic and determination.

Here is a koan with acted-out answers designed to set the ball of play in motion:

MASTER

It is said, "To pick up a stone from the bottom of the deep Ise Sea without even wetting your sleeve." How do you understand this?

ANSWER

The pupil pretends to jump into the ocean and bring up a big stone.

MASTER

What is this stone called?

ANSWER

The pupil gives his own name.

MASTER

About how heavy is this stone?

ANSWER

The pupil gives his own weight.[45]

To jump into the water without getting wet, to plunge to the bottom effortlessly, to forget yourself so that you are one with the stone being picked up, to know that a distinction between self and other, subject and object, can be overcome—all these insights are possible when you let both the ridiculousness and the humor of the koan overpower you. The ball of play is passed back and forth between master and student. The Taoist sense of motion and flow is acted out. The moves are sometimes swift, sometimes deliberate. To be sure, koan work is serious business, but it is nonetheless a game in which the humor of the situation can lead to a breakthrough.

Often a humorous person or situation is for Zen people the revealer of the quality of life known as *mushin,* or "no mind." In addition to the three laughing sages of Tiger Ravine, five comical eccentrics have been the subject of much Ch'an and Zen writing and painting: Fen-kan, a probably late-eighth-century wanderer and owner of a pet tiger; Kanzan (known in Chinese as Han-shan, meaning "Cold Mountain"), a ninth-century carefree, clowning frequenter of Ch'an communities; his companion Jittoku (Chinese, Shih-te, "Foundling"), a humorous, unpredictable doer of chores in temples and elsewhere; Hotei (Chinese, Pu-tai, "Cloth Bag"), an early-tenth-century, pot-bellied traveler among villages and companion of children; and Ryokan, an early-nineteenth-century folkdancer and games teacher of the Japanese Soto tradition. The jokes, bizarre clothing, intriguing faces, comical gestures, dances, play, and body movement of these five "divine fools" all demonstrate the free spirit of *mushin.*

Kanzan and his like-minded friends live in "no mind" because they have let go of attachment to persons, things, and institutions. Not being controlled by anything outside themselves, they relate to all things spontaneously and indiscriminately. They live in a sense of wonder about everything; they give themselves to all people and to all tasks. They have appropriated the meaning of the saying: "Wonder of wonders! I haul water, I hew wood." They live inside the Zen insistence on other simple matters: "I play, I eat, I dance, I sweep, I laugh." They move ecstatically through a world where, paradoxically, everything is relevant and nothing is relevant. They are living out *mushin* in their preoccupation with what is happening at the moment; they practice no mind through the wonder of "everyday mind."

The five Zen clowns are also understood to practice *mushin* because of a rare joining of confidence and innocence. In one delightful painting Kanzan is poring over a scroll with a gleeful look in his eye; the scroll is blank; and it is said that Kanzan could not have read the characters even if they had been there. He is spoofing those who depend for knowledge of the Zen way upon extensive sutra reading. But his humorous antic means more. Soon he will join his friend Jittoku in sweeping out a temple room "where, in the beginning, there was not even a speck of dust."[46]

> Reading sutras Kanzan does not
> understand their meanings,
> Reciting poems he does not know
> their rules
> Holding a broom Jittoku does not
> remove dust,
> Pointing to the moon, he does
> not forget the finger.[47]

These wise fools will try anything, even things they cannot do well, or things that might not seem necessary, in confidence that the wholeness of the Zen person does not depend on the measurements of scholarship, memorization, and work schedule. Innocently and with childlike enthusiasm, they will engage themselves. They will not claim expertness in their many pursuits; indeed, they will question any glorification of expertness on the part of others.

In Zen, one way to practice *mushin* is to attempt many things, rather than strive compulsively for standards in a few. Zen uses humor to proclaim the necessity of a "primary naiveté"—to use Paul Ricoeur's phrase—a joyful, spontaneous, uncritical response to activities and situations. When one has the innocence and confidence of wanting to try anything, one is then ready for a "secondary naiveté," at which level the primary responses are incorporated into some kind of structure. According to Zen, there is no point in functioning in a structure—practicing a religious discipline, learning an art, studying old Chinese in order to read sutras—unless the ordered pursuit builds on an ever-present primary naiveté. Throughout all function and activity, one should be like the *dharma* mirror, which, by its nature, is able to reflect and take in many things.

Lastly, humor is important in Zen because of its corroborating power in the *sangha,* or the Zen community. Humor, Zen people would say, is different from wit. The latter is often used as a demonstration of ego and as a means of competition with others. Humor, whether delicate or boisterous and guffawing, brings to human awareness a matter than can be perceived by all—something that is already in the public domain. Humor is readily infectious because its subject matter is something potentially known. Humor expresses a common human situation and, in so doing, invites persons to discover what is already true about themselves. Wit is not invitational; rather than producing bonds among people and calling them to participate, wit creates adulation, sometimes awe, often jealousy, and usually distance. Wit is a talented performance; humor is a shared job. The master who clowns at lunch during a sesshin, or dances after dinner, or who laughs over tea about stories of aching legs and knees is asking others to share his antics, his movements, his pain, his boisterousness. He is not using his comic ways to lord it over the members of the *sangha* or to ask for their admiration. He is asking them to join in.

Humor in the Zen community is also protective. By dealing with the common human situation and by inviting participation, the comic spirit of Zen offers a feeling of acceptance to members of the group. A hedge of protection is raised against insecurity, the sense of not being wanted, and inferiority. Humor calls the members of the *sangha* to join together in the creation of a special bond among themselves.

Suzuki Daisetz has said that "Zen is the only religion or teaching that finds room for laughter." [48] It is true, at least in degree. No other religious perspective is so preoccupied with the comic spirit—Zen has humor embedded in its art, poetry, painting, anecdotes, lectures, and even its discipline. For Zen people, humor is the very salt of both humanness and religion. The teachings can only be known in the presence of a comic spirit—a creative force which shapes the crucible out of which much of the Zen way emerges.

Samadhi: Things together

An exploration of the word *samadhi* offers a final way of considering the meaning of Zen. An important Sanskrit word of varied meaning for Hinduism and Buddhism, *samadhi* is known in Japanese as *zammai* or *sammai.* It can mean balance or harmony; the term can also refer, particularly in Mahayana Buddhism, to a person's disciplined state, to powers of concentration, to "one-mindedness," to a *wei wu wei* ("doing without doing") kind of effort in any activity. But its root significance, at least for most Zen people, is a description of a state of heightened and expanded awareness. The person who lives in samadhi has the mind of the Zen mirror, which takes in all things and sees interconnections naturally. The awareness of a Zen person is known first in her ability to see all objects and experiences as having a significance in the present. Her personal history is not to be lived in or dwelled upon extensively. Dependence on the future and projections are also understood as containing unreality and even deception. Zen is uneasy with nostalgia; she who longs for a physical or psychological homeland lives as a sojourner in the present. Likewise, Zen teaching does not foster a longing for a special time that is to come. There is no "Pure

Land" to be awaited, some future condition or place of reconciliation and fulfillment.

Ryokan, one of the Zen comic spirits mentioned before, made a stunning calligraphy of the two characters for "heaven" and "earth." The brush strokes are impetuous; they run together in abbreviated, uninhibited style. Ryokan seems to stress that the worldly and celestial flow into each other—that the two cosmic opposites are joined—and must be represented now by two connected strokes. He concludes with a dot, as if to say *sumimashita,* or "finished" or "so be it." In Zen there is no transcendent reality or heavenly place or condition beyond this present life and what is happening now. True to the teachings of Mahayana from the time of Nagarjuna, the Indian philosopher of the second century A.D., Zen has maintained that *samsara,* the ongoing journey through the relativities of life, is *nirvana,* the experience of peace and changelessness. To think of it another way: The Buddha is not awaiting you in some place and time; rather, in the words of a traditional Zen teaching, "Apart from your person now, there is no Buddha." Oemaru says in haiku, making light of a coming nirvana and a future Buddhahood:

> Squatting like Buddha:
> But bitten
> By mosquitoes
> In my nirvana.[49]

So a Zen person mindful of the events of the past and aware of the possibilities of the future concentrates on the reality of the moment. Samadhi is associated with an ever-expanding consciousness of what is taking place before one's eyes.

Secondly, a Zen person grasps the meaning of the term

when, in individual activities, there is a sense that parts and functions go together to make a whole. The awareness is known when an athlete, an artist, a poet, a lover has "contact with a unity more real than the apparent complexity of things."[50] A practitioner of aikido experiences samadhi when his turns, dodges, and movement are of one pattern and occur without transition. When a person learns a craft, he is at first conscious of the many different steps necessary in his art. But then, as proficiency increases, he becomes unconscious of parts and consciousness attaches itself, rather, to the total process of the craft.

A third meaning is found in the Zen insistence that one can be united with an object. A lover of the Japanese stringed koto or of the Zen *shakuhachi* flute can become so identified with what is being heard that she may feel that there are no segments, such as listening, music being listened to, and listener. There is simply music without subject or object. A similar comment can be made about viewing objects of great beauty. Through the eye's use of *kensho,* the art of seeing into the nature of things, the self can become united with a particular flower. Zen would insist on the abiding particularity of self and flower, but it would say that in the dynamics of viewing and beholding there emerges a sense of being joined to the object. Self and flower are like the blue mountain and the white cloud mentioned earlier—independent, but, in the process of true seeing, they depend on each other and are one. This is akin to the Zen understanding of love. A parent merges with a child, a husband with a wife, a lover with a lover, a friend with a friend. While they maintain difference and uniqueness, out of the acts of relationship and the ongoing struggle of closeness there emerges a fusing and a unity. Samadhi relates to the sense of being joined to something or somebody else while knowing particularity—of being aware that in the dynamics of hearing, seeing, or living out a relationship there can be unity.

Lastly, samadhi as a Zen quality relates to death and dying, a matter to be amplified in the next chapter. Living is living and death is death—the particulars will not be denied. But in the dynamics of self-reflection and consciousness there is a sense that all people are engaged in living-dying and dying-living. Or, as a Zen saying has it, "Life and death are like two sides of the same piece of paper—try to separate them."

Samadhi, with all its meanings, is what one experiences in satori, enlightenment—that particular moment in practice or activity when the point of Zen comes in with a rush. Samadhi, with its concentration on the moment, its emphasis on the coalescence of parts and activities, its insistence on unity emerging out of particulars when a process is underway or a relationship experienced, is a summing-up term. Zen refines and elaborates the advice of chapter 22 of the *Tao Te Ching,* "Be really whole, and all things will come to you." Samadhi in Zen refers to a particular kind of wholeness which stresses the reality of parts and objects, but affirms, nonetheless, that one can live in a connected, undifferentiated world.

Zen is not primarily a philosophy, certainly not a doctrine. A roshi would much rather talk about what it is to "do" Zen than about what it is. In fact, the advice often given those who ask about the meaning of Zen is: Do the simple thing at hand. "If there is rice, eat it; if there is tea, drink it; if there are cushions, zazen." If one does the thing at hand with sensitivity and concentration, the meaning of Zen will be grasped. To do Zen means not only to participate fully in present tasks of "hewing wood and carrying water," but to be in a discipline where moments of awareness are repeated and one is involved in a rhythmic search for meaning. An often-repeated Mahayana phrase is "Mind, having no fixed abode, should flow forth." But only in a discipline will the mind flow forth—leaving behind projections, frustrations, and the entrapments of personal history—and move to look in the *dharma* mirror, where emptiness, interconnection, and nonduality are grasped.

It is said that a Zen temple is an observatory for inner space. Concentrating on the *hara* region in zazen, sensing unity in one's own body, searching for harmony, "bringing the world into the self," all point to the profound inner dimension of Zen. One can be joyful over what one finds. Basho said:

> I will not forget
> This lonely savor
> Of my life's
> One little dewdrop.[51]

Zen accomplishes the voyage to inner space in a special way. All faculties must be used—the intellectual, the emotional, the physical. All techniques and disciplines are to be guided by the spirit of humor, which has symbolic and transforming power. Abe Masao suggests that Zen expresses itself through "raising one's eyebrows and winking one's eyes."

The voyage is not one-way, however. One returns from inner concentration to function effectively and compassionately in the world of work, decisions, ambiguities, frailties, and violence. One does not go to the observatory for inner space at the expense of other people. Abe also states that Zen is "working to save others at the crossroads." [52] The purpose of Zen training is often described by roshis as the disciplining of self for the benefit of others. Only when a participant is passionately concerned about the *sangha*, or the community, both at hand and at large, is he able to enter into the Zen spirit.

Many people, especially those in affluent America and Japan, lack nothing, yet they feel themselves to be lacking. Zen is ruthless in its insistence that we examine what we have and what we depend on. It urges us to cut away and to discard, so that the true diamond of the self may emerge. In this sense, Zen is a beneficent destroyer. Long after its migration across China and the Sea of Japan, Zen still maintains a closeness with one of the ancient Indian gods. Shiva the "Destroyer" is implicitly honored in the practice and symbol structure of Zen. This is the Shiva so often portrayed as casting aside and destroying the nonessentials of life and then dancing and rejoicing.

To be empty, to enjoy silence, to do zazen, to accept a discipline, to be egoless, to live in the comic spirit, to use the body, to have a special esthetic, to follow the compassionate way—these are the marks of Zen.

Notes

1. Henry S. Hughes, *The Obstructed Path: French Social Thought in the Years of Desperation, 1930–1960* (New York: Harper & Row, 1968), p. 5.

2. Webster Schott, "Poet of the Age of Anxiety," *Life*, 30 January 1970, p. 54.

3. Shibayama Zenkei, *A Flower Does Not Talk* (Tokyo: Charles E. Tuttle, 1970), p. 264.

4. The literature on Zen is, of course, voluminous. If I were to recommend only a half dozen books in English, they would be the following: Heinrich Dumoulin, *A History of Zen Buddhism*, trans. Paul Peachey (New York: Random House, 1963); Jan Fontein and Money L. Hickman, eds., *Zen Painting and Calligraphy* (Boston: Museum of Fine Arts, 1970); Philip Kapleau, *The Three Pillars of Zen* (New York: Harper & Row, 1969); Shibayama Zenkei, *Zen Comments on the Mumonkan*, trans. Kudo Sumiko, pref. by Kenneth W. Morgan (New York: New American Library, 1974); Suzuki Daisetz, *Zen and Japanese*

Culture (Princeton: Princeton University Press, 1959); and Suzuki Shunryu, *Zen Mind, Beginner's Mind* (New York: John Weatherhill, 1970).

5. Hubert Benoit, *The Supreme Doctrine: Psychological Studies in Zen Thought* (New York: Viking Press, 1957), p. 105.

6. Shibayama, *Flower,* p. 81.

7. The four "holy truths" are: a pronouncement that transitory, human existence is evil and produces unhappiness; an analysis that unhappiness is caused by desire; a promise that unhappiness can be stopped; and a method set forth in the eightfold path. The eight ways in which desire and selfish craving, or *tanha,* can be destroyed are: right understanding or vision, right purpose or aspiration, right speech, right conduct, right vocation, right effort, right alertness or mindfulness, and right concentration.

8. Takeuchi Yoshinori, "The Silence of Buddha," *Philosophical Studies of Japan* 6 (1965): 45 and 58, two quotations.

9. Dom Aelred Graham, *Conversations: Christian and Buddhist* (New York: Harcourt, Brace and World, 1968), p. 146.

10. On her Jaffrey, N.H., tombstone, being a quotation from her *My Antonia.*

11. Suzuki, *Zen and Japanese,* p. 231.

12. William Theodore de Bary, Donald Keene, and Tsunoda Ryusaku, eds., *Sources of Japanese Tradition* (New York: Columbia University Press, 1958), 1:246.

13. Tange Kenzo and Kawazoe Noboru, *Ise: Original Form of Japanese Architecture* (Tokyo: Asahi Shinbun-sha, 1962), p. 166.

14. Basho, *The Narrow Road to the Deep North and Other Travel Sketches,* introd., trans. Yuasa Nobuyuki (New York: Penguin Books, 1966), pp. 87, 94, 133, 33.

15. Nancy W. Ross, *The World of Zen* (New York: Random House, 1960), p. 23.

16. Shibayama, *Flower,* pp. 76–77.

17. Suzuki, *Zen Mind,* p. 27.

18. Chang Chung-Yuan, *Creativity and Taoism: A Study of Chinese Philosophy, Art, and Poetry* (New York: Harper & Row, 1970), pp. 56–57.

19. See H. Ganse Little, Jr., *Decision and Responsibility: A Wrinkle in Time* (Tallahassee, Fla.: American Academy of Religion, 1974).

20. Dumoulin, *History,* pp. 76–77.

21. *Cherry-Blossoms: Japanese Haiku,* Series III (Mt. Vernon, N.Y.: Peter Pauper Press, 1960), p. 50.

22. Paul Wienpahl, *Zen Diary* (New York: Harper & Row, 1970), p. 73.

23. Tange, *Ise,* p. 11.

24. Christmas Humphreys, *Zen Comes West: The Present and Future of Zen Buddhism in Great Britain* (New York: Macmillan, 1960), p. 33.

25. Suzuki, *Zen and Japanese*, p. 232.

26. Shibayama, *Flower*, p. 42.

27. See Trungpa Chogyam, *Meditation in Action* (Berkeley: Shambala Publications, 1970).

28. *Daily Sutras for Chanting and Recitation* (New York: New York Zendo of the Zen Studies Society, 1970), p. 2.

29. Alan Watts, *The Way of Zen* (New York: Random House, 1957), p. 142.

30. Kapleau, *Three Pillars*, p. 169.

31. Philip Kapleau, "Is Zazen an Escape?" *Zen Bow* 2, no. 4 (August–September 1969): 2.

32. Gary Snyder, *Wind Bell* 14, no. 1 (Summer 1975): 16.

33. Trungpa, *Meditation*, p. 15.

34. Ken Yasuda, *Japanese Haiku*, (Tokyo: Charles E. Tuttle, 1957) p. 6.

35. Harold Stewart, essay and trans., *A Net of Fireflies: Japanese Haiku and Haiku Paintings* (Tokyo: Charles E. Tuttle, 1960), p. 122, both haiku.

36. Conrad Hyers, *Zen and the Comic Spirit* (Philadelphia: Westminster Press, 1973), p. 35. Hyers rightly urges that the "Zen of Pu-tai" (the Ch'an clown, known in Japan as Hotei) be considered as fundamental in the tradition as "Bodhidharma Zen."

37. "Rinzairoku," *Daily Sutras*, p. 55.

38. *Cherry-Blossoms*, p. 58.

39. Paul Wienpahl, *The Matter of Zen: A Brief Account of Zazen* (New York: New York University Press, 1964), pp. 43–44.

40. Harold G. Henderson, commentary and trans., *An Introduction to Haiku: An Anthology of Poems and Poets from Basho to Shiki* (Garden City: Doubleday, 1958), p. 147.

41. Reginald H. Blyth, *Oriental Humour* (Tokyo: Hokuseido Press, 1959), p. 226.

42. Hyers, *Zen and the Comic Spirit*, p. 33.

43. Paul Reps and Senzaki Nyogen, eds., *Zen Flesh, Zen Bones* (Garden City: Doubleday, n. d.), p. 65.

44. Suzuki Daisetz, *Sengai: The Zen Master*, ed. Eva van Hoboken (Greenwich, Conn.: New York Graphic Society, 1971), p. 103.

45. Yoel Hoffmann, commentary and trans., Sojo Hirano, foreword, Ben-Ami Scharfstein, intro., *The Sound of the One Hand: 281 Koan with Answers* (New York: Basic Books, 1975), pp. 22, 72, poem and koan.

46. Fontein, *Zen Painting*, p. 113.

47. Sengai colophon, Idemitsu calendar, 1975.

48. Suzuki, *Sengai,* p. 11.

49. *Cherry-Blossoms,* p. 22

50. Arthur Waley, *Zen Buddhism and Its Relation to Art* (London: Luzac, 1922), p. 26.

51. *Cherry-Blossoms,* p. 30.

52. "Zen and Western Thought," *International Philosophical Quarterly* 10, no. 4 (December 1970): 526, both quotations.

Jittoku, or Shih-te in Chinese,
attributed to Yen Hui.
A Chinese Zen or Ch'an comic spirit.

Courtesy of Museum of Fine Arts, Boston, and Tokyo National Museum.

Three

THE JOURNEY TO ZEN

The impasse is opened and a new vista
    presents itself . . .
Everything taking place here is no other
    than the Buddha-life itself.
                    The Six Ox-herding Pictures

So Abram went up from Egypt, he and his wife,
and all that he had, and Lot with him, into
the Negeb.
                    Gen. 13:1

"Pine needles forever green"

In the main room of the Tea Ceremony Society of
Urasenke in New York City, presided over by Yamada
Hisashi, a *kakemono,* hanging scroll with calligraphy, is always present. One of my favorites often found in the
tatami (straw mat) room translates "pine needles forever
green." When my students and I asked Yamada-sensei
about the meaning of the calligraphy, he remarked that
just as pine needles never lose their green color, so we as
individuals should never lose what we have—we should be
what we are. We should not try to add other colors, false
and inharmonious, to those which we naturally have. We
should present ourselves as we are. The meaning of "pine
needles forever green" is "you as you."

More than anything else, Zen has taught me not only to

accept myself but to rejoice in whatever stage of life I find myself. I came to Zen in middle age. I found it speaking to me about the many problems that plaque the forties and fifties and beyond—yearning for younger days, change in physical appearance and function, weariness over continuing in the same job, fearful over the productivity of the last part of one's career, and wondering about death. Zen has helped me to see myself and my activities in a new way.

Bhagwan Shree Rajneesh, a frequent commentator on Zen stories and sutras, tells of a woman who was very pleased with a delivery boy's promptness and thoroughness. She decided it was high time to find out his name. When asked, he replied, "Shakespeare." "Well, that is quite a famous name," she said. He came back, "It should be; I have been delivering in this neighborhood for almost three years now."[1] There are good and fulfilling things occurring in what I am doing right now; I do not need to be somebody else or do something else.

This new approach has been helped by grasping the Zen emphasis on "real nature." My true self is never destroyed by delusion or anxiety; nor is it exalted and made into something else through rigorous discipline and even enlightenment. My real nature is waiting to be discovered genuinely and entirely in all my experiences, moods, and conditions. It is present in the voids and abysses as well as in the peaks of discipline, joy, and productivity. In the T'ang dynasty, a Ch'an practitioner came to see master Zenne of Kassan and asked, "How are things?" The master answered: "Just as they are." The words used in the reply were *yomo* or *shimo,* meaning "as it is," or "in its suchness." Zenne was expressing his self-realization, or his serenity and good feeling, about who he was and about what he was doing.[2]

Zen has helped me to understand and present myself as

I am by making it easy to enter its way. In the introduction to the *Mumonkan,* the *Gateless Gate,* a Zen koan text, is found a key statement: "The Great Tao has no gate. There are infinite ways to reach it."[3] The Way can be entered anywhere by anyone; it has no prerequisite or required preamble. A Zen counsel on beginning is, "Enter where you are." Initially my beginning came about not through participation in zazen, but rather through a need in my own life for directness and unadornedness. I had long been attracted to functional art forms, based on simple lines, plainness, and subtlety. Shaker furniture had increasingly held my attention and admiration. For me, zazen and mind-body training were to follow a study of sparse Zen gardens and beginning attempts to construct this Zen art form. I began to work with angular "mountain rocks"; small, gray white stone, raked in simple patterns; and blank space. It was a genuine entrance, arising out of my interests and needs. Others will cite different entrances, for the great Tao *is* gateless.

The Zen way has given me assurance because it stresses the importance of each moment and experience. It has said to me, more clearly than anything else in my life, "Pour yourself into what is happening now, for it will not happen again." A famous tea man, Ii Naosuke, a feudal lord known for both his justice and his power, once said that tea ceremony was *ichi-go, ichi-e*—one time, one meeting. Those gathered together for tea would never meet again under precisely the same circumstances. The meaning of the ceremony is to capture the particular significance of what is transpiring at this moment in one's thoughts, of sharing with others in this setting, and of taking in these sounds and tastes. Zen says that each moment should be like a tea ceremony. It will not come again. Fullness and meaning are to be sought after right now.

Zen has helped me rejoice over who I am and what I am doing by speaking of the new that is always happening. Another tea-ceremony expression, often placed on a *kakemono,* is *totsu, totsu.* In a literal sense, this expression means a "clicking"—perhaps a clucking of the tongue—a recognition of something that suddenly seems different, even strange. *Totsu, totsu* is an exclamation and statement of surprise. One should be prepared not only in the event of tea ceremony but in all moments for new ideas, new attractions, new developments "around the corner." For many years I have played baroque and classical music on clarinet and recorder. Recently, in the Zen spirit of new things—and through the influence of my children—I have come to enjoy good country music and bluegrass. I find that my mediocre dexterity could be put to use in improvisation and harmony for folk and bluegrass with guitar and fiddle. Playing with a group—and playing with records—has been a kind of *totsu, totsu* for me.

Contentment with the present stage of my life and what I am has been possible, in part, because of the Zen stress on self-expression. Zen encourages genuine inquiry about feelings and an expression of them. In all pursuits, one is urged to practice directness and avoid subterfuge. In the tea ceremony, in the very midst of the formalities, one has the freedom to speak, as well as the greater freedom not to speak. One freedom is not better than the other; each has its place, if pursued genuinely and thoughtfully.

Zen encourages people to be, do, and express what they feel in their bodies. We once took our children to the Kyoto, Japan, zoo with its extensive and well-designed yards, cages, and pools. As we were leaning over the seal tank, very close to those graceful creatures slithering on rocks and darting through the water, one of our sons said, "I'd like to be a seal." A Zen friend who was with us on the outing thought this an imaginative, insightful remark. We talked about its meaning. Our son expressed something which I, as a swimmer, have always wanted: to be like a seal in the water, moving limbs efficiently, going easily from air to water and back again. Swimming has always been an important activity for me, but ever since this remark and following conversation I have thought afresh about "sealness" and about the way to express such a quality in body motion and technique.

Insistence upon self-expression and assertion of feeling is based on the Zen point that true self-understanding can lead to world or "outside" understanding. A sensitive artist is able to express that which is felt by everybody. To be profoundly subjective is to be revealingly objective. The more we express ourselves genuinely, the closer we come to the *dharma,* or underlying reality.

Zen has helped me see that the more sincerely I express myself, the closer I come to others. My real nature is not my limited, falsely structured ego; rather, my true nature encompasses and stretches out to other people. The famous "Ox-herding" tableaux reveal this central insight. Ten small paintings (or six, in another rendition) depict the Zen seeker searching for his "true mind," represented by a strong, crafty ox. The seeker sights the ox, tracks it, finally tames it, and then rides it in such a fashion that ox and seeker are one. In order to capture the ox, the seeker must know his true desires and needs. He must express them and be honest about them. The last scene shows the seeker entering the market place, grinning and striding with confidence. The caption reads, "Without recourse to mystic powers, withered trees he swiftly brings to bloom." The principal meaning of the withered trees is a reference to discouraged, anguished, suffering other people. The ultimate meaning of self-assertion and expression of need and

desire is to serve others and bring them "to bloom." In
Zen, I have found this sequence to be true in my own life.
When assertive about my genuine needs and desires, I am
ready to help others in therapy, lecturing, counseling, writing, and preaching. I become authentic and whole, and
more of me is ready to listen, advise, teach, and do whatever is at hand.

Practice

I entered Zen through a need for simplicity and directness in my life and through a responsiveness to a certain
kind of beauty. At the beginning I dimly grasped the
meaning of my journey. It was not until I entered the
practice of Zen that meanings became clearer and more
abundant. The way of Zen came to have illumination and
power when I became involved in zazen, chanting, mondo,
a new sense of using my body, and a deeper understanding
of esthetics.

In zazen, I first discovered that quietness and removal
from appointments, meetings, books, telephone, office,
and people were invigorating. I often thought of myself as
a cat at the beginning of my experience with zazen. The
world of noise, smells, and sights may be whirling about,
but cats and other animals can crouch still "in the midst of
things." They seem to be preparing themselves for what
may soon require energy and action. At the very beginning
I felt this sense of preparation for what would soon be
upon me. I began to understand why cats are favorite sub-
jects of Zen painters—intact, solidly poised, sometimes
wrapped in a ball, restful, making ready for future happenings.

An early book on Zen for me was Hubert Benoit, *The
Supreme Doctrine: Psychological Studies in Zen Thought.* Be-

noit speaks about the necessity of immobilization in the animal and insect world. Only when a caterpillar is overtaken by the seeming stagnation of being a chrysalis is it able to begin the process of becoming a butterfly and living a new life. Stillness and immobilization are not to be feared or shunned; rather, such states are indispensable to functioning and development.

In the beginning, zazen appealed to me because of its complete simplicity. I did not need to have a mantra, a special word or phrase, secretly given to me; no images were to be placed before my eyes or kept in my mind with eyes shut. Rather, I was instructed to put aside all forms, objects, and thoughts; things were to leave my mind rather than enter during practice.

Zazen next came to have a meaning of deep self-encounter. At the beginning stages of my practice, I had to deal with diversions; fantasies about sex; thoughts about my marriage, my children, my job, even my death; and the ever-present list of "things to do today." Psychic conflicts, unrecalled for years, appeared in a genuine and frightening way. I remember one sitting when, up from somewhere, came in sharp detail the derisive words I had used in teenage arguments with my mother. For a time I relived an acute Oedipal ambivalence, carefully suppressed for many years. Later, as a result of practice, I believe, I came to understand better both my need for closeness and sharing with my mother as well as my need for separation and independence.

Early experiences in zazen taught me to accept all feelings and thoughts as a genuine part of myself. If I had only my mind to work with during zazen, I certainly must accept and use it totally. I began to welcome this entrance of thoughts and feelings. No matter how startling or shattering a fantasy might be I took it in. I looked at all the

impasses to concentration and asked what they were telling me about myself.

Gradually, as a next step, I was able to let thoughts and
all diversions go through me, as Zen masters advise, without questioning at length their significance. They *were* me
but they had to be let go in order to make a deeper self-
confrontation. Not an easy task! But I began to see that my
distractions and fantasies were, after all, "occasional
phenomena"—even epiphenomena, fluttering on the surface like leaves in a current. I tried to work directly on my
mind, on the depths below; if I could still the deeps, the
surface action would cease. If you wish to know what
somebody else is saying and who they are, you have to stop
talking and listen. Thinking is talking inside your head. I
tried to stop thinking so that I could listen to and find my
true self.

How to stop thinking? Concentration on breathing and
counting breaths did not automatically bring me to a Zen
"place." I often had to do something to quell the pulses of
my thinking self. In the early stages of my practice, and
frequently since, I began a sitting by employing the powerful symbolism of Shiva the Destroyer, the Hindu god
whom many Zen people honor. Shiva destroys so that the
new may come; Shiva dances away the old and exults;
Shiva removes things so that vision may focus more deeply
and sharply; Shiva takes away obstacles so that mind
and spirit may move in a different way. I used, and still do,
as a preface to zazen, a simple, singable three-line Shiva
chant:

>Om
>Nama-ah
>Shivai-aya

It means "Inexpressible reality and unity (Om), hail and praise (nama-ah) to Shiva (Shivai-aya)." It sounds better than it reads!

Confronting myself in thoughts, distractions, fantasies, and outcroppings of the unconscious—and welcoming these as part of my true self—were beginning stages for me in zazen. Letting these things go was, and is, a harder step. Concentrating directly on my mind and its potential stillness is harder yet. At no step along the way has the discipline been easy. Many sittings have been and still are battles; I have struggled with drowsiness, pain in the knees, and uncontrollable wanderings of mind. But gradually and unpredictably, I have come often to a good place. There has been an emptiness of body and mind—perhaps it might be described as a sense of ongoing, uninterrupted suspension. "Above the cushion there is no person, and under the cushion there is no person, and under the cushion there is no floor."

A Japanese saying about practice is *Jiki shin kore dojo,* "A pure, straight, honest mind is your place"—or even "training place." The words refer to the purity of the place of nothingness, interconnection, and nonduality; they assert that Zen practice can be pursued anywhere. But they also speak, at least to me, of the straight and honest way of encountering myself as a precondition to any understanding of zazen. Emptiness, suspension, and other characteristic terms about meditation are not grasped in zazen until I take confrontation with myself seriously and instructively. When Dogen had returned to Japan from five years of Ch'an practice in China, he was asked what he had learned. He is said to have replied: "I know nothing, except that my eyes are horizontal and my nose is vertical."

When a good Zen place is reached, I find that I am concentrating on what is happening at the moment. I enter into the ebb and flow of my breathing, the sequence of counting, the enjoyment of stillness and "time out," the support and confirmation of those doing zazen with me. No matter how much I may know about Zen, I do not think of the books I have read or the arts I have pursued; rather I concentrate on what is unfolding—or, as it is sometimes put, "How it all is." I feel myself to be a vehicle, a conduit, through which *ki,* energy, is flowing. I sense *ki* going from me to the outside, but I am also aware of *ki* coming back to me. As with breathing in and out, or tides in a great bay, I am conscious of energy and force leaving me, but only to reenter. The going and coming are not separate, but depend on and need each other and form one process.

To concentrate on what is happening means eliminating judgments and opinions about other people, about problems, and even about my practice. I am not asking about the purpose of sitting, nor do I seek to discover a validation of zazen which could be offered to others or to myself. Dogen's phrase, "Practice is enlightenment," puts the emphasis aright. The purpose of zazen is to do what I am doing. I do not feel that I am heading for some goal or insight. Rather, I am at once practicing and I have also arrived. Before a sitting and in between sittings, I have used with a teacher, and later with my students, an early Mahayana chant: *Gate, gate; paragate; parasamagate,* Gone, gone; gone beyond; gone beyond beyond. I try to cross over and leave behind judgments, reflections on ends and purposes, questions about whether to sit or not to sit.

Let me mention two mondo sayings, haikulike in their imaginative terseness, which have helped me enter a place of *gate, gate* during sittings. The first is connected with Zen's insistence on suchness, taking and seeing things "just as they are." It states, "The flowers are red; the willows are green." Concentrating on willows and greenness and then flowers and redness—and associating one with inhalation and another with exhalation—has often put me beyond opinions, judgments, and questions. The saying "In my bamboo hut this spring, there is nothing; there is everything" has been even more helpful. It has allowed me to focus on the possibility of my mind as Buddhamind and therefore possessing everything. It also places "everything" and "nothing" beside one another and equal to each other. "Nothing" can be the mode of exhalation and "everything" the mode of inhalation, stressing that nothing is given to the world and that everything comes from the world. The association can also be reversed so that one's Buddhamind is sensed as "everything," going out to the world during exhalation, and "nothing" can be associated with inhalation. And then, if focusing and concentration are functioning, the mondo can be left behind and "gone beyond" is reached without need of saying or reference.

Some individual sittings I can remember; others I cannot. The ones remembered are not better than the ones forgotten—they are all part of the same practice. One sitting clearly remembered, which has illuminated later zazen, occurred during a weekend sesshin with my students. Along with other parts of Zen discipline, we were doing zazen at dawn, noon, dusk, and midnight. The sitting in mind was at dawn; the clappers and bell sounded while it was yet dark. I began chapter 1 with a reference to this sitting—now let me add slight detail. I did not speculate on the purpose of our gathering; I did not even ask why I came in from moonlight skiing to begin zazen. I was immediately caught up in the enjoyment of silence and simplicity of our procedure. I seemed to be emptying my mind as legs were folded and abdominal breathing began. I did not use the Shiva chant or the helpful symbolism of the "bamboo hut" mondo saying. I sensed how the stillness of the time just before dawn matched the silence of our sitting. I was aware of the gentle spreading of light, and finally of the sudden brightness of a winter morning. I felt energy flowing through me—the *ki* of the coming day entering, as well as energy going from me to the world. I sat content with being a channel. I was simply and totally there in the midst of everything that was happening.

And now a final meaning of zazen for me. While seemingly individualistic and solitary, the practice of zazen has come to have a communal and even a compassionate sense. Although the purpose or aim of zazen should be put aside during a sitting, masters will occasionally speak or ask about the reasons for meditation during a discussion period. Many answers can be given and many are correct: to gain quietness, to know unity, "just to sit," to be like a mountain, to lose one's ego, to find one's place. Many masters, including Shimano-roshi, the teacher with whom I am close, adds that the purpose is to "have the mind of the compassionate *bodhisattva*"—a heroic, enlightened being who helps others.

The more I sit, the more I am aware of and appreciate the meaning and significance of others. I become aware not only of the problems and doubts of those sitting with me, but also of their singularity and uniqueness. I grasp special things about my wife and my children; I am led to consider individual students rather than confront a class. A rekindling of interests in social issues and action often occurs during periods of extended sitting. One zazen group began a campus-wide collection to support orphaned and wounded children in Vietnam during the aftermath of the war. All of this takes place, I believe, because zazen breaks down the isolated concept of the self within whose confines we live most of our lives. This breaking down is connected in meaning with the Zen insistence on genuine self-expression. Rather than going outward in order to understand the self, zazen calls you to go deeper into yourself. The more sustained and thorough the journey into yourself, the more you find yourself joined with others and with the whole universe.

A remark of Kobori-roshi of Ryoko-in, a subtemple of Daitoku-ji in Kyoto, may serve as a conclusion to this section. He says that at the end of zazen he always feels "very fresh, very fresh." Except for standoff battles with sleepiness, I would confirm Kobori-roshi's words. Even after a long struggle with distraction and even after pain in the knees, at the end of a sitting I am quickened and restored. I not only have the feeling of being ready to rise and return to the world of appointments, classes, preparations, writing, meetings, and counseling, but I have the sense of going back easily. The boundary between sitting and activity is not sharp or rough; I feel that I glide smoothly over the line. Ultimately this means that zazen for me is not just confined to periods of sitting, but furnishes energy and perspective which are with me between sittings. To practice zazen is to be made fresh.

The use of the body in Zen discipline has a twofold meaning for me. In the first place, the proper use of the body has a connection with zazen; and, secondly, physical activities by themselves take on new form and meaning in Zen. I have found it important to be involved in hatha yoga, exercises of stretching and flexibility, in order to prepare my back and legs for zazen. The image of bamboo is meaningful to have in mind as one does yogic or other bending and flexing exercises. Bamboo branches do not snap and break in the wind or under the weight of snow; rather, they bend and give to let the wind pass through or the snow slide off. I tried Zen archery and aikido in Japan and at home, but time has not been available for concentrated work in these disciplines. Rather, I have tried to focus on sports and activities in which I have had some experience and which do not require a master-student relationship. All of them, however, require practice and the help and insight of a good teacher or coach.

Swimming, running, and cross-country skiing have taken on special meaning because of my interest in Zen. These three, done in the company of others or alone, have direct connection with the practice of zazen. Each one emphasizes relaxed and natural breathing; each one calls for endurance, breaking through a barrier of discomfort and distraction to reach an inner space where extension and continuity are possible; and each involves, even in the briefest span of time, a sense of being empty, a pouring out, a feeling of untying physical and psychological knots.

I find that other aspects of these activities are indirectly connected with the practice of zazen. Just as in sitting one should be aware that all one's parts are functioning together—head, neck, back, loosely folded hands, supporting tripod of legs and buttocks—so a swimmer, runner, or cross-country skier is aware of the coordination of the parts of her body. A runner must not forget that the swing of her arms and hands must match the stride of her legs. A swimmer must not only be able to move water with her arms, but also fit the moment of breathing and an ongoing kick into that movement. All three of these sports require a sense of rhythm, natural and unexaggerated, such as the rhythm necessary in zazen as one takes in air through the upper body to the *hara,* or the abdomen, and then releases it. Each of these sports calls for participation in a field of energy, or *ki,* finding it in yourself as well as in the world about you as you keep going in the water, or on a path or track, or over snow. There may be many other physical activities which have these qualities associated with Zen insights and the practice of zazen. Rowing, canoeing, cycling, rock climbing, and kayaking are such, I believe. Many sports, however, do not have the link with Zen—especially those which rely on a charged competitive spirit between teams, stop-and-go action, and body contact with opponents. Such sports certainly do involve concentration and coordination and therefore have some connection with Zen, but they contain few parallels to zazen and generally lack a Zen spirit.

On a snowy, cloudy March Sunday I started on a long cross-country ski race in Sweden known as the Vasaloppet. In the predawn darkness at the beginning of the race, many of us in the nine thousand present wondered if we would be able to complete the eighty-five-kilometer course. We would be doing only one thing that day: skiing to Mora, now many kilometers and hills away. During the morning, I enjoyed the good snow, the up and down of the terrain, the well-laid-out track, the tundras, and the frozen lakes. When I was at the halfway point, a person ran up to us on the course and announced that a hometown skier from Mora had just won the race, prevailing over Olympic skiers from Russia, Norway, and Finland. My legs were already tired and my breathing irregular—and this news, with half the course to go, immediately made me feel worse. The afternoon wore on, and I began to feel that I would never finish. But then something happened; there was a changeover inside me; a door opened into a space of new energy and insight. Residents of a small town along the course generously gave me hot soup and rolls, as well as the traditional blueberry drink. Most important, I began to think anew about myself in the midst of this strange venture. I had come this far and I was not falling down or lying in the snow; mind and body wanted to go on—far better to ski to the end than give up or be asked to leave at a checkpoint and ride to the finish on a bus. I stopped fighting the uphills and began simply to accept them. I thought of the *ki,* or energy, that was all about me in the cries of "Heya, heya" from those who were urging on me and others in the world of moving clouds and blowing snow. I began to do slower abdominal breathing. During inhalations I thought of taking in the *ki* about me and making it part of my body. I appropriated the energy and applied it to aching thigh muscles and stiff back and shoulders. I began to think of lengthening and stretching. I began to work on a better coordination of poling and striding, and then not thinking about it. I tried to ski in the spirit of Taoist *wei wu wei,* doing by not doing, not racing. Most of all, I went through the last third of the course trying to empty myself of all thoughts of oncoming darkness, tiredness, reasons for and against continuing, kilometers, pain, the long way already come, and the section ahead. I tried to concentrate on what was happening now. I listened to the sliding and swishing of my skis and to my breathing in and breathing out; I stayed within the sounds of these rhythms. I was not trying to beat others or finish more kilometers. Rather, all of me was caught up in what was taking place at each moment. I turned the last part of the race into a form of meditation and suddenly, in the darkness of early evening, I was crossing the finish line.

Physical activities, and especially these three, have a broader connection with Zen. They are not only associated with zazen, and zazen with them, but each has a general Zen significance. Basho's classic haiku reads traditionally in English:

> The ancient pond,
> A frog jumped in—
> Plop.

Bhagwan Rajneesh comments that the first two lines totally run together in Japanese and should read in English "ancient-pond-frog-jump-in." [4] The path for the runner, the water for the swimmer, and the snow for the skier are not "out there" or "over there"—just as the ancient pond is not out there or set apart for the jumping frog. Path, water, snow, and you are connected when you are involved in your activity. The Zen significance of these sports is that the connection can be perceived and taken in. Your motion and the stillness of path, water, or snow are part of the same *dharma,* or abiding reality. "Plop" stands for a recognition of this unity, a translation of the line *mizu no oto,* sound of water. Once again, Zen asserts that data and phenomena—in this case, places and physical activities— are identifiable and separable, but that while engaging in certain pursuits a sense of belonging and "joinedness" emerge. Just as "ancient-pond" and "frog-jump-in" belong together on one line, so "winter-woods-road" and "I-skion" can be grasped together and at once. A snow-filled February trail calls a cross-country skier; he feels as if he should be there, and once on it he feels that he and it are joined. So runners feel about favorite routes and swimmers about special bodies of water. "Plop"—and we grasp the deep connection between ourselves running, swimming, skiing and a place.

There is also in these sports, and I am sure in others, too, the Zen sense of exaltation. You move for the sheer joy of movement. You swim for the feeling of moving like a seal at the moment. You run and cross-country ski for the exhilaration of going over a surface as smoothly and effortlessly as possible. In these activities, you cut yourself off from fragmenting divisions of schedule and jagged arrangements of daily life to see yourself as a whole, acting in one piece. This use of the body offers not only a special kind of joy in motion and a sense of being whole; it also leads to freedom and a spirit of abandonment. Zorba, the Greek who loved to dance, caught this Zen spirit when he warned his boss: "You're on a long piece of string, boss; you come and go, and think you're free, but you never cut the string in two. And when people don't cut that string. . . ." [5]

Lastly, an immersion in Zen esthetics has been an important part of practice for me. It has never been difficult to appreciate Zen concern for simplicity, subtlety, and naturalness, as seen in woodblock prints, calligraphy, brush-and-ink drawings, and in the general use of form. This appreciation, as stated before, was my "way into" Zen. More recently, I moved from the position of an observer and admirer to that of a maker and participant by working with students in making three Zen gardens. They were patterned, all too inadequately, after the famous rock, stone, and sand "dry gardens" of Myoshin-ji, Ryoan-ji, and Ginkaku-ji in Kyoto. Each visit to these temples had provided me a moment of insight, as well as an occasion for seeing something new. Each session of working with a Japanese Zen gardener had been a filled and special time.

Two of the gardens were built in the sheltered corner of a yard under the branches of an old plum tree and the third against the background of a stone wall made out of foundation rock from an old New England barn. *Yama,* or mountain type, rocks were used in the gardens asymmetrical, jagged, and rugged in appearance. The beds of the garden were crushed small stone from a nearby quarry. The plum tree had been pruned to provide an overarching cover, but not to dominate. An odd number of standing rocks and stepping-stones across the middle were used to carry out the Zen theme of a break from too neat an ordering. Nothing grew in the three small gardens, except moss which had begun to climb the shady side of some rocks and on the stone wall. As one stands or sits beside this art form—so different from our usual conception of a garden—one's eye is attracted to the angularity and the particulars of each rock, but it is also called to the black space and "emptiness" of the small expanse.

The *sangha* experience had immediate significance for me. The long hours of digging and preparation, the discussion about the right kind of stones and rocks, the raking of appropriate simple designs in the bed, and the continuing care of the garden produced a bond among us. We encountered and dealt with each other's assertiveness about shape and design; we worked long hours (in the rain and under the moonlight); we seemed to grasp the *ichi-go, ichi-e,* one time, one meeting, character of the project. There would not be another time when we particular individuals would share our ideas so honestly, search genuinely for a consensus, laugh, and create. We seemed to be participating equally in the event, not following the usual pattern of foreman and workers.

Second, the making of the garden became a work of both mind and the hands. We read about Japanese gardens, especially about Zen arrangements; we looked at slides and diagrams; we studied the history of particular gardens and even the lives of certain designers. In one of the gardens, the largest upright stone, placed off center— gray, rough, heavy, angular—came from the excavations for a college library. We reflected on the fact that the site of its origin would house all manner of things pertaining to the mind. But then we also dug, moved stone, arranged and rearranged, raked, generally exhausted ourselves. We chose the principal stones for the garden on the basis of what we had read and what I had learned in Japan. We kept in mind the connection between zazen and "mountain" shape rocks, remembering that masters frequently say, "Sit like a great mountain." In the midst of the emptiness of the garden the large stones stood symbolically for mountains (but they were also to be perceived nonsymbolically "just as rocks"). We chose the stones on the basis of our first impressions of them in their original locations, their appearance as we viewed them in the sunshine and in the rain, and the way they felt when we moved them and worked with them.

The making of the garden was an intellectual and sensory task. We went back and forth between the two modes of understanding beauty. Our work seemed to fit a section in the "Guiding Principles" of the Zen society I joined at the subtemple Reiun-in, "Spirit of Cloud Temple," at Myoshin-ji in Kyoto: "We guard against the powerlessness resulting from onesided attention to intellectual study alone, and against the blindness resulting from onesided attention to practice alone. Thus, combining study and practice into a single act, we proceed." Throughout, we knew that books were books and that digging was digging; but we also knew that the two went together and could hardly be separated in our project. The unity of two separate and distinct functions became apparent, in Zen style once more, in an actual task or process.

Third, building the two gardens reaffirmed for me the importance of being in the midst of beauty. It is a Zen insistence that we understand and take in meaning from direct experience, not from observation and viewing from afar. Zazen is to be done, not read about. Running is to be engaged in, not talked about. The particular beauty of the gardens for us emerged when we were immersed in digging, placing, and carrying. After completion, the gardens spoke their meaning when we were raking them, sitting beside them quietly, or showing them to others. On a plum-blossom morning, or on a rainy afternoon, or on a clear night—or at any other particular time—the Zen beauty of these places became pervasive as one walked slowly across or stood beside them for a time. The garden could be thought about, but its meaning came through when one was in it, working on it, or alongside it.

Zen insists that we enter into the specialness of each object in order to understand its beauty. We are to go wherever beauty is, sensing it and feeling it. A cold winter's night calls us to go outside and participate in it, even momentarily. So Taigi suggests in his haiku:

> Every single star
> Is quivering now
> With light . . .
> O how bitter cold.[6]

The comic

Humor has been my teacher along the Zen path. Masters know that alongside rigor, structure, and discipline there must be a sense of "something different," even a feeling of reaction to practice. Zen has, in my experience, always proclaimed the delicate balance of structure and antistructure. The ironic, the boisterous, the absurd, and even the cavorting are necessary complements to zazen, work with mondo, and physical discipline; one goes back and forth continually between structure and antistructure. I have found that to practice Zen without smiles, infectious laughter, rolling on the floor is to do an incomplete and deadening thing.

Once, at the end of a long early morning sitting, my foot went to sleep. When the bell rang, I knew I would not make it to my feet to bow to my zazen associates of the day unless I rubbed and massaged to get circulation going again. Many others, I noted happily, were doing the same thing to various parts of the body—but not my very close neighbor, a few inches away, a resident of the community and an experienced sitter. He had decided apparently to remain in zazen posture until the very last moment. Then he would rise as we Mahayana masseurs and chiropractic Zen neophytes began to struggle to our feet. I massaged the ankle for what seemed a very long time, but the numbness continued; I decided to look down and see if my ankle was even there. I turned and, to my embarrassment, discovered that I had been rubbing my neighbor's ankle. He looked at me and then began to smile and finally to chuckle. I did the same—a little more slowly than he, however. He helped me to my feet and we continued to exchange gulps of laughter as we did gassho, bows of gratitude, to our fellow members. Drinking green tea following kinhin, walking after zazen, our eyes met occasionally, and there was continued response to each other. The incident took me abruptly from structure to antistructure. It also made me aware, naturally and suddenly, of a sense of closeness with a person I barely knew. Humor had, in likely Zen fashion, placed before me the possibility of relatedness and of *sangha*.

To tell another story, my students and I were invited to a traditional breakfast following a morning sitting. After prayers, chanting, and serving food, a special plate was passed among us as we sat on the floor around a low table. Each person was to place a morsel of her hot cereal on the dish. The plate with the small pieces would then be placed in front of the statue of the Buddha as an offering; later, the dry pieces would be taken into the garden for the birds. Interest and curiosity ran high as the special dish made its rounds in silence. Everyone, beginner and expert, entered into the ritual. However, students at the far end of the table somehow got the idea that the pieces of cereal were to be taken off the plate and added to their own bowls. By the time the dish came back to the roshi, presiding at the head of the table, there were very few pieces left. There was a long awkward moment—and then the place broke up with wide-eyed stares, smiles, giggles, and English and Japanese utterances of "Oh!" and "*So, ne!*" Again, humor had suddenly brought us out of structure into antistructure. But other Zen points emerged. We were laughing at our own procedures and rituals; there was no proclamation of righteousness because some had done the correct thing, separating them from those who had not; the Buddha was being presented with nearly an empty offering plate, which only stressed that he is not to be worshipped anyway or petitioned with gifts.

Comic situations and jokes are, to me, important models or paradigms for a Zen understanding of a good "place." To enter into a humorous event or to be able to laugh at a story requires turning aside, seeing things differently, letting the moment engulf you. The turning, seeing, and letting parallel Zen methods in zazen and mondo. The "I get it" response to a joke or the quick revelation in a humorous situation are helpful analogies to the abrupt perception known in *kensho,* the art of seeing directly into the nature of things—including seeing into yourself.

The Buddhahood of all things

Zen concern with particulars is based on a belief that individual things have their own specialness and that this specialness is to be honored. There is no hierarchy of value among the things of this world, with human beings somehow residing at the apex, lording it over all. A Chinese saying, often mentioned in Taoist and Zen tracts, is *Shan te shan; shui te shui*—Mountain gets mountain; water gets water. The startling thing about a mountain is that it is so much like a mountain, and water so much like water.[7] A person knows and appreciates a mountain when massiveness, angularity, and changing hues are known; and water when motion, sound, and reflection are known. The Zen tradition calls us to discover, respect, and enjoy the marks of particularity and to sense a completeness and value in each thing as it is. Our wonder is to be directed not towards *how* something is or *whether* it is better than something else, but *that* it is. Zen, along with the whole Mahayana tradition, affirms the "Buddhahood of all things." This Buddhahood is grasped when we search for and identify the meaning and worth of the particular and try to comprehend its myriad ways.

Our family spends its summers in the "North Country" of New Hampshire, where we live in a small mountain town located at the foot of the Presidential Range. Our summer life of study, vacationing, writing, climbing, swimming, and working is dominated by the specialness of the peaks, valleys, and rivers of this part of the White Mountains. In many ways, Mount Washington, being the highest point in the northeastern United States, dominates our surroundings. We live at the foot of Mount Madison and Mount Adams, a few miles from Mount Washington and other Presidential peaks. I have had many good skiing and climbing trips on Mount Washington, but in the last few years I have become increasingly unhappy over developments on the mountain. Many, many people are on its trails during the summer; a good April or May weekend will find hundreds of skiers in Tuckerman's Ravine; an ancient cog railway clanks to the summit, belching out black smoke along one of the ridges; an improved "carriage road" allows automobiles to reach the top with ease;

and a small commercialized village caps the mountain. Long ago, I made a resolve to stay away from Mount Washington and find mountain pleasures elsewhere. Somehow, this great peak had lost its soul.

But here we are, summer after summer, living in the Mount Washington Valley, and there the peak is with its impressive summit cone, its valleys, and its ridges. During a recent summer, I began to wonder how well I really knew Mount Washington. Had I made a judgment too quickly? During July and early August, I thought about the meaning of a Zen saying: "At first, I thought I knew what a mountain was and what a river was. Then I felt I did not know what a mountain was and what a river was. Now I know what a mountain is and what a river is." The saying can be a description of stages of life as well as a mondo for meditation. The words began to apply to my thinking about Mount Washington. It occurred to me that I was in stage two: I did not know what Mount Washington was. What did I know about its specific Buddhahood? It seemed to be losing its soul, through no fault of its own, but did I really know what its soul was? What could I do to understand Mount Washington in a new way?

My brother David and I began to discuss a way of rediscovering the mountain. We decided to spend an entire day on Washington, beginning before dawn and ending after nightfall, ascending and descending, going up and down and across the mountain using different routes. Our hope was that we would come to know the mountain *sono mama*, just as it is, leaving behind our judgments and opinions. Perhaps we would be able to climb Mount Washington several times, although we had no goal. We would just be there for a long mountain day—continually moving while observing, discussing, discovering, and "seeing into." As it turned out, we climbed the mountain three times. We began on a mid-August day just before 5:00 A.M. under a setting full moon, and we finished at 8:00 P.M. in the wind and the rain.

As we started in the cold under the moon, occasionally using a flashlight in the dense woods, we were probably the only people moving on the mountain. It seemed to be our mountain as we climbed in the early morning through a great ravine and came to the top, watching dawn break on the peak, and the valleys fill with light. But, as we began our first descent, the glories of a sun-filled August day called people to the mountain by the hundreds—on the trails, the cog railway, and the carriage road. Suddenly, we were two among many. At the end of the day, however, when we began our last descent, we saw no one else on the summit cone. And as we walked down through Tuckerman's Ravine to Pinkham Notch, through weather changing to scudding clouds, rain, and gusty wind, we met only three National Forest personnel hurrying to make camp before dark.

My brother and I had gone back and forth between a "people phase" and a "no-people phase" of the mountain. In the dim light of dawn, the mountain seemed alone, awesome, and very much itself. But we were surprised that these qualities continued even in midday. The people who came to Washington were, in fact, on it for a very short part of the day. The mountain seemed to welcome those who were there for those brief hours, and then seemed to return happily to its lonely self for the long hours of dusk and night. We came to have an appreciation for both phases—when the mountain was with people, and the greater time when it belonged to itself. Something of its goodness and character were there all the time.

We became aware of the mountain's massiveness and variety. As we went up and down and across during the day, we appreciated anew the extent of the ridges connecting adjoining mountains and the broadness of the high plateau land. We contrasted the steepness of the ravines with the gentleness of lowland forest paths. The ruggedness of Mount Washington came through to us in a new way. We discussed signs recently put up by mountain clubs: "Respect the mountain; some day she will demand it." We understood that warning as we descended Ammonoosuc Ravine in the sunlight without shirts, but on a later descent elsewhere put on all the clothing in our packs as wind and rain caught us. We found that on this day we were on both a midsummer mountain and an autumn mountain. We commented on how differently the same ravine, trail, and rock field looked now in moonlight, now in sunshine, and now in clouds and rain. Lastly, as we gave ourselves to the mountain that day, we discovered new things about familiar places: large clumps of Labrador tea in a boulder field above the tree line; smooth, straight places in a well-known trail; a miniature spruce flattened against the lee side of a big rock at a resting place; unnoticed parts of neighboring ranges seen from favorite vista points. On the way down, we noted the open beauty of a particular alpine plant at midday; later, on the way up for the last time, we saw it closing as it made ready for a night of growling wind and driving rain. A pair of white butterflies flitted about the summit at 1:00 P.M., but later at the top the temperature had dropped and the butterflies were gone. The meaning of the mountain came through in those fifteen hours. The specialness of Mount Washington was beginning to be understood by simply observing, being on it, and letting it declare its own Buddhahood.

We had other experiences on the mountain that long August day. They were not directly connected with the Buddhahood of all things, but associated with Zen insights. In order to understand the "suchness" and particularity of the mountain while moving on it continuously through its day, we drained ourselves physically, emotionally, and mentally. The wisdom of taking something "as it is" only came through an emptying of ourselves as the day wore on. When the afternoon became early evening and we wondered if legs and lungs could carry us farther, we ceased to think of ourselves and concentrated on the mountain. As in the Vasaloppet experience, thought went only to each mountain moment. Early in the day we gave up discussing objectives or trying to think about them; we didn't know whether we could climb the mountain three times or not. We began to see that the meaning of the experience was not to concentrate on a goal or an end, but to grasp the significance of what was unfolding at each hour and minute as the mountain went through its day. Indeed, only when we thought about one moment simply following another were we able to enter into the mountain's Buddhahood. In this spirit we continued and made the day not a contest with the mountain but a time of its self-revelation to us.

As in the case of many other experiences, there was a connection with zazen. I thought of a very long sitting once at the New York zendo; I was wondering if I could make it to the end. Suddenly, Shimano-roshi broke silence and said loudly, "Endure, endure." I came back with a jolt to the moment and its significance and cast the goal of finishing away. Also, as in a sitting, I went back and forth during that mountain day between a sense of solitariness and a sense of sharing and being with others.

We gained a strong sense of identity with the mountain during the course of the day. Washington was going through its daily hours from dawn to nightfall and displayed its summer and autumn phases to us. My brother and I were not conscious of time, but very conscious of space on the mountain—ravines, trails, outcroppings, high plateaux, and forests. Slowly and majestically, without going anywhere, the mountain went through time on that August day. Slowly and unmajestically, we kept moving on and through its space, up and down, checking maps, not stopping for meals, usually eating as we walked. Our spatial movement matched the chronological movement of the mountain. One of the abiding memories of the experience is that "mountain-time" and "we-space" went on together and each was a part of the other. The unity between the mountain and ourselves on that day reminded me of the Zen poem mentioned earlier about the geese, whose fast flight represents time, and the pond, whose area stands for space. When the reflection of the geese is caught by the water's surface, time and space come together in one instant. We sensed the fusion of time and space in that long day on Mount Washington.

While we came to affirm the Buddhahood of the mountain and that "A mountain is a mountain," we also discovered that "A mountain is not a mountain." Washington is not a mountain in the sense that it is part of a whole series of ridges and other mountains, part of the Appalachian chain, part of a long geologic process, part of the whole cosmos. The water from a spring at the top of one ravine trickles and then tumbles down to become the broad flowing Ammonoosuc River in the valley and lowlands, joins the Connecticut, and finally reaches Long Island Sound and the Atlantic. We saw the mountain in its particularity, but we also saw it in its connection with countless other places and forces. By seeing that the massiveness on which we spent our day was a mountain but also not a mountain, we sensed the identity of contradiction present in Zen.

Let me return to the idea of Buddhahood and mention an environmental aspect of the day's experience. My brother and I became aware of the mountain's specificness, its aloneness, and its character. But we also saw the erosion on trails from hundreds of hikers, litter at the summit, and black smoke from the cog railway on the ridge. We saw afresh what people were doing to the mountain. The Buddhahood of all things means that no one form of existence may heedlessly and destructively impose its desires and ways on another. It means respecting all forms of existence. Buddhahood demands that people blend their wants and needs with the specialness of natural things surrounding them. We are a part of nature, not above it and not dominating it. Human beings have their own uniqueness, but they are to live in the midst of other forms of vividness. As we climbed up and down the mountain that day, we talked about not only the character of Washington, but also about responsibility and vigilance.

The Buddhahood of all things calls us to search for ways which will allow things to be as they are supposed to be. The particular character of rivers, mountains, and trees should require us to look for and cherish the life force and the spirit of these natural things. The wife of Kobori-roshi, master of Ryoko-in, a subtemple of Daitoku-ji in Kyoto, was once seen pouring *ichi ban no sake,* choice rice wine, on the roots of a pine tree in the garden. Asked why she was doing this at the foot of the tree, she smiled and said, "To keep it happy."

Caring and giving

I mentioned before the saying of Oda-roshi, Gary Snyder's teacher: "Zen is two things, meditation and sweeping the garden." I interpret "sweeping" in this summary statement to mean paying attention to the body and using it; but, in an equally important sense, it is also a reference to compassion. Cleaning up, being mindful of others, caring for people and things beyond one's self are fundamental parts of the Zen way. In the San Francisco and Tassajara Zen communities of California, Suzuki-roshi, Baker-roshi, and members have long insisted on caring not just for the natural objects of their farm and mountain community, but for people caught in inner-city problems and frustrations. The publication *Wind Bell* speaks of the Zen community's concern for "absentee ownership and real estate exploitation, declining local business, redlining by financial institutions, high unemployment and crime rates, no post office, library, or adequate recreational facilities." [8] Establishing cooperatives, offering counseling services, and organizing work parties are an expression of Zen compassion. More of this concern may be found in America than in Japanese Zen communities. But I have observed monks, lay members, and novices from Daitoku-ji cleaning up the banks of the Kamo River in order to make those potentially attractive areas a better place for children to play in the crowded northern section of Kyoto.

One of my unforgettable American Zen experiences consisted of several visits to the Museum of Fine Arts in Boston, the sister city of Kyoto, when an exhibition of "Zen Painting and Calligraphy" was held. I remember standing in front of the exquisite calligraphy in the form of a Buddhist hymn by Tao-lung Lan-ch'i (1212–78). Tao-lung, a native of Szechwan in China, came to Kyoto and Kamakura as a young, highly respected teacher. He was the first to be awarded in Japan the title *zenji,* or Zen master. Part of the hymn reads: "May we open our compassionate hearts to relieve those who are in peril or in want." While concerned with inner personal peace, Tao-lung prays that "The land within the Four Seas may live in peace and harmony without even one arrow being shot." And he concludes his calligraphy with the hope that "Tranquility may reign inside our temple gate; that peace may prevail inside as well as outside." [9]

Nearly all periods of zazen and Zen services begin with some form of the vow of the *bodhisattva,* a heroic being who promises to save all others before entering nirvana. The ideal of the *bodhisattva* in Mahayana Buddhism is very different from the ideal of the *arhat* of Hinayana Buddhism, one who commits himself to attaining his own enlightenment. In Reiun-in, "Spirit of Cloud Temple" at Myoshin-ji, we would begin each zazen with these words in Japanese: "However innumerable beings are, we vow to save them . . . [Let us] become fully compassionate humans, make total use of our gifts according to our respective vocations in life, discern agony both individual and social and its source." We pledged to each other that we would "partake of the honored work of creating the world."

Caring for animals and all manner of things nonhuman is part of Zen compassion. To be sure, this kind of caring is practiced by many who have never heard of Mahayana compassion. The particular Zen quality of such concern is the extension of tenderness toward all things. Wherever distress and suffering are known—whenever something cannot be what it is supposed to be—there the Zen spirit applies. One is not just concerned about the furry residents of one's own household or the brook in one's backyard. Issa, the haiku poet who identified himself with many things animate and inanimate, wrote:

> Lean frog,
> Don't give up the fight
> Issa is here! [10]

Zen makes a connection between compassion and our understanding of giving. So often we consciously or unconsciously emphasize our act of giving—reveling in our generosity, frequently expecting something in return, or at least an acceptable response from the receiver. Parents usually give gifts to their children with great strings attached. Mothers and fathers, paying the high cost of education, will often say to their seemingly rebellious student offspring, "After all we are doing for you, you go ahead and do this!" The Zen advice is to prepare your gift carefully and lovingly, give it joyfully, and then forget it. Giving has nothing to do with expectation—or, worse yet, with manipulation. A giver should see things passing within the same *ki,* or energy field, or totality of being. Giving is like passing something from the right hand to the left, Zen folk say—the object is moved, but remains within the whole organism. To draw a line between bestower and receiver is to make a sharp subject-object dualism. The spirit of giving should also be coupled with nonattachment. If one follows what he gives with expectations and demands, he is attached still to his gift. If I make a ceremony out of my giving and stress that something which was "mine" is now "yours," I am attached to my own distinctions and ritual of giving.

In an intensive winter study program on "Zen Discipline," students and I engaged in bread making. As we made bread for each other and for people outside the group, we began to share our recipes freely—even our own "special" ones. We came to sense nonattachment to our techniques and formulae. The words in the front matter of the *Tassajara Bread Book* took on meaning: "A recipe doesn't belong to anyone. Given to me, I give it to you."

Compassion arises naturally and easily from discipline and practice. In discussion over green tea following zazen, a suggestion came spontaneously from students that we should collect money and help to organize programs for the relocation of southeast Asian children in our Berkshire community. And so it was done, quickly and unobtrusively.

Caring and giving are seen in Zen as directly associated with relatedness and self-need. The giver, the receiver, the gift, and the act of giving are all connected and depend on each other. What we give to others is not only part of a whole, but is likely to come back, for nothing is ever sent away or set apart. Soen-roshi speaks bluntly about the interconnection in the case of the gift of encouragement and enthusiasm: "If you want to get encouragement, you should encourage others." [11]

Death and dying

My journey to Zen has given me a new understanding of my own end, the dying of others, and the meaning of death itself. Zen does not hide death; it speaks freely and emphatically about the inevitable. In *sumi-e,* brush-and-ink drawing, both the Taoist and Zen traditions use blankness and "empty" space to focus attention not only on the bamboo, the cat, or the heron being presented, but to remind the viewer of her own blankness, annihilation—her *mujo,* or impermanence. In Zen, one is called upon not only to accept death but to speak about it openly. The speaking is not to be done in hushed voice, nor is it to be accompanied by fanfare. Why should there be special treatment for something that is always present, awaiting every person, something so natural? Unlike other Chinese and Japanese sages who offered philosophical "death poems," Basho refused to compose final stanzas. He preferred simply to refer to the fact of his impending death:

Never giving thought to fame,
One troublesome span of life behind,
Cross-legged in the coffin,
I'm about to slough the flesh.[12]

Basho also told his disciples, "I have no particular farewell poem. The poems which I have composed day by day are all my farewell poems." [13] Ryokan caught the simple inevitability and naturalness of death in his haiku:

Showing now its front side,
Now its back,
Falls the maple leaf.[14]

Death is ordinary, but it has its own poignancy and power. Death changes things. Joyful people become mourners; longing replaces fulfillment; there is a before and an after. Zen takes grief and sadness over the death of others seriously. It speaks of understanding and compassion for those going through separation from others. It urges the mourner to be honest and to express his grief. Onitsura wrote a haiku for the anniversary of the death of his child:

Rising autumn moon . . .
Lighting in my
Lap this year
No pale sickly child.[15]

And Basho again writes movingly, this time about a mourning father:

Deep under ashes . . .
Burning charcoal
Chilled now by
His hissing tears.[16]

Even anxiety over one's own death, a foreboding sense of separation, a fear that one may not be able to see what one's children will become—all these personal death feelings are understood in Zen and are to be spoken of in honesty and directness. The particular is again affirmed by Zen. There can be no denial of the sharpness, the angularity, the finiteness, the abruptness of death.

But there is also the insistence that in and through the experienced particularity there abides an innate connection with something else. A death event, or feeling or thought about death, like the single blossom in an array or an isolated stone in a garden, is associated with more. The "more" is the unity of life and death. Zen teaches, along with other perspectives, but more emphatically, that there is no dying without living and no living without dying. The practice of *kensho*, the art of seeing into the nature of things, means that something can only be known in the presence of something else. The wind is not seen, but trees and branches moving back and forth show it to be present. Figures and objects in a painting stand out and have meaning only because of surrounding blank space, and emptiness in a painting is only meaningful because of figures and object. Dying is known only because of living and living because of dying. No dualism can be present. As mentioned before, living and dying are like two sides of the same piece of paper, which cannot be separated—more than that, we *are* that sheet of paper with its two sides of life and death. At any moment we are all life and all death. As Dogen says in the *Shusho-gi, Discourse on the Training of Enlightenment,* "Within life *and* death, there exists Buddha." [17] There can be no attachment to either, but only a recognition of living-dying and dying-living.

In Zen ceremonies marking death, living and dying are meaningfully put together. Abe Masao invited a group of us, Japanese and Americans, to visit a memorial place for Nishida Kitaro in Reiun-in at Myoshin-ji in Kyoto. Nishida, a leading contributor to the modern Kyoto School of Buddhist philosophy, died in 1945 in a Zen monastery in Kamakura, watching the fires set by the last bombing runs on Japan. His ashes reside in three locations, one of them being Reiun-in, "Spirit of Cloud Temple," where he had often practiced. In Reiun-in, the memorial place is marked by a stone about six feet long, shaped like a gently rolling mountain ridge. On the face of the stone is carved simply Nishida's pen name, given to him by a Japanese Zen master, who, in customary practice, had taken the name from a Chinese poet. Two slender flower arrangements were in front of the stone. We were all silent as we stood in a half circle, overarched by trees in the garden and the massive Myoshin-ji temple bell. Then Abe-sensei poured water on the rock from a bamboo dipper. He smiled and said that he was doing this to the memorial stone "to keep it alive." He invited all of us to pour water, and so we did until the whole rock was glistening. We stayed a little longer in silence, bowed in gassho, gratitude, and left for our zazen in the main hall of Reiun-in. Nishida was dead, but we all felt we had marked his livingness.

When Suzuki-roshi died at Tassajara in California in 1972, those invited to the memorial ceremony received a simple card which read:

> A ceremony will be held at Tassajara
> Sunday, October 22, 1972, at 2:00 P.M.
> to place the ashes of our teacher
> Shunryu Suzuki-roshi in the ground.
> Please attend if you can.
> There will be a dinner after the ceremony.

Death, ashes, hole in the ground—but also dinner, celebration, *sangha* or community. There is death in life but also life in death.

My father died of cancer of the liver several years ago at Thanksgiving time. It was a sabbatical year for me and there was opportunity to see him and talk with him as his life came to an end. My father was a Christian minister whose imaginative and dedicated career of preaching, counseling, and community service was influential in the lives of countless people. I am one of those persons. Whenever I make a speech or give a sermon, I always think of his natural, direct, expressive style; whenever difficult problems arise in counseling, I think of his probing, yet gentle way of dealing with people. Christian though he was, I believe that a Zen spirit was present in his dying. As I think back on our conversations and recall his interpretation of what was happening, it is clear that he affirmed the particularity of his death. He knew he was dying, although he and I seldom spoke of that fact; he knew that he was in great pain; and he knew that the particular end that was coming was not the way of dying he would have chosen. But he had already accepted the approach of death. He was free to speak about himself and his family, the events and news of the day, the present happenings in the lives of others. Knowing that death was soon to come, we both concentrated on the many dimensions of this "now." We never spoke of heaven; we never discussed immortality; we never talked of a "great divide."

My father was living out his dying. Only a living person can die, but it is also true that only a dying person can live. Every moment became important to him. We are all beings-toward-death, but each step along the way has its own meaning. My father had always been fully involved in each step of his life, and now he was dying the way he lived. Philip Kapleau of the Zen center in Rochester, New York, had called this saying to my attention: "A man who dies before he dies does not die when he dies." I mentioned the gist of these words to my father, and he nodded. And, once again, we began to speak of what was taking place now. His living and his dying were joined.[18]

cf. Psalms

When death did come, there was sadness and there were tears. But most of all there was—and is—the continuing presence in my mind and heart of a man who really knew about living and dying and their inseparableness. At the simple, stark moment when the news came, I hummed a favorite hymn, said a family prayer, and reflected on Sora's haiku:

> On the last long road
> When I fall and
> Fail to rise . . .
> I'll bed with flowers.[19]

Zen has helped me to think about my own end in a new way. Indeed, it is the one thing that has made it possible for me to think at all about my dying. For years, my death was not to be pondered; others die, but not I, the runner, swimmer, cross-country skier, hiker, and climber—not I, the one who is in full strength. I would minister to others about their end, but never to myself. Zen has urged me to listen to the pulses of life and the stillness of death that are joined in myself. The words of a friend interested in Zen, written for the memorial service of his father and read by me as minister, have stood in my mind. "He seemed to pursue time with such delicacy." Knowing that I am a living-dying person, I have come recently to have a delicate sense about the passage of time. It means not only making the hours count. It means that when I listen to the dying that is going on in the midst of my living, I have a chance of casting aside pretensions about myself. I let go of fantasies about the present; I give up impossible designs for the future. I am trying to be simply what I can become. A sense of authentic living has come as I think about myself as a being-toward-death.

Zen has helped me think about the whole process of aging and has suggested new patterns of ministering to others at a time of death. Youth, vigor, strength, and physical attractiveness are gods today in the culture of both the West and East. Comely bodies and faces catch our eye on magazine stands and television; articles on how to stay youthful abound; the glorification of the "young set" is found in Tokyo and San Francisco, Kyoto and Boston. An attractive, recreational ocean inn on the Sea of Japan in Wajima is called "The Young Inn"; hostels for the young and those on "youth trips" are plentiful in Europe and the United States. In contemporary culture, East and West, it is almost embarrassing to contemplate seventy-year-olds who hike or ride bicycles. Not only do we shun the looks and pursuits of senior people, but we fail to concern ourselves with the contribution of older folk in our midst. We overlook their ability to listen, arising from the fact that they have heard much and are receptive; their wisdom, gained through long experience with both destructive and fulfilling elements of life; their response to human dilemmas, coming from hard-earned knowledge that personal decisions are seldom simple and clear-cut.

We also do not place, especially in the West, any value on that which lies beyond aging—death itself. Fading, losing strength, drawing closer to the end are not to be discussed; rather they are to be feared and ignored. A traditional Japanese poem speaks about three matters of great value:

I have seen the moon and the blossoms; now I go
To view the last and loveliest: the snow.

The moon stands for mystery and differentness, the cherry
blossoms for beauty and renewal—but what of the snow?
Yuki, the word for snow, has in Japanese a homophone
which means "going." The snow has dazzling and trans-
forming beauty in its cold stillness; it also reminds us of
our frailty when it gusts and blows through a long winter
night. But, for most Japanese, snow symbolizes more than
physical aspects. It stands for cold death and points to the
purity of the void, where all distinctions fade and where all
directions are the same—as if one were a snow-blinded
hunter. There is a saying, *Yuki no hate wa nehan,* "After
the snow comes nirvana." [20] The "last and loveliest" on our
living-dying journey may be death. At the end, we are
going to the void, the supreme place of all good places—
where craving ceases, peace is present, interconnection
abides, and dualism is no more. The nirvana of death,
according to Zen, is a state of *fusho-fushi,* unbornness and
undyingness. [21] In death, we no longer have to go through
anything; we are already beyond the process and change
known in this life. Chuang-tzu, the Taoist poet and
philosopher, once asked two powerful questions: "How do
I know that love of life is not an illusion after all? How do I
know but that he who dreads death is not as a child who
has lost his way and does not know his way home?" [22]

Rather than see death as a necessary marking or place on
our living-dying journey, we view it as a frightful abyss.
Rather than understanding our movement toward death as
a "way home," we conceive it to be a road into the camp of
the enemy. It is not connected with our living and our
consciousness. It overcomes us; we do not let it be a part
of us. We have made it an outside force which strikes us

down. We say of a person who is very sick, "She *has* to die"; rather than noting simply that she is dying, just as we are living. She is at one marking in living-dying and we are at another.

When death occurs, Zen has helped me, as a Christian minister, deal with its presence when ministering to others. Rather than skirt the subject, I now talk freely about death's sharpness and devastation with bereaved family and friends. In the case of a tragic accident to a young person, or even in the awaited death of an ailing older person, the "hissing tears" of Basho are to be shed by all, including myself. I encourage those in physical and spiritual distress over the death of another to speak about the dying and the living of the person now gone. At the time of an ending, we now have a chance to grasp the truth that we are all beings-toward-death. The moment of death also becomes an occasion when we may speak to each other about our own living and dying. Sometimes it is even possible to console one another with humor about the everydayness and ordinariness of death. A Zen story tells of an ailing abbot who, in the middle of the winter, decided that he had outlived his usefulness and would starve himself to death. When asked by his monks why he refused his food, he replied that he wished to die because he had only become a bother to everyone. They told him, "If you die now when it is so cold, everybody will be uncomfortable at your funeral, and you will be even a greater nuisance, so please eat!" He began eating again, but when spring came he once more stopped and not long after died.[23]

To speak about and listen to the expression of our living-dying unity, to comfort, to help the love and support of others to be present, to plan for a marking or ceremony—these have become my tasks in ministering to others. I no longer speak of heaven, for heaven clouds over and covers up what is taking place on earth.

So, good things have happened to me in my journey to Zen. The story of the journey is still unfolding, for new meanings continue to be found. I happily make the journey each time I do zazen, work on a rock-and-stone garden, sense the rhythm and surroundingness of *ki,* energy, in my body, participate in the revealing insights that only come from humor, learn to know what a mountain really is, and think in new ways about death. It is an ongoing journey of understanding and joy.

Notes

1. Bhagwan Shree Rajneesh, *Rajneesh Foundation Newsletter* 2, no. 7 (1976): 6.

2. Shibayama Zenkei, *A Flower Does Not Talk* (Tokyo: Charles E. Tuttle, 1970), pp. 206–7.

3. Shibayama, *Flower,* p. 32.

4. *Rajneesh Foundation Newsletter* 2, no. 7 (1976): 5.

5. Nikos Kazantzakis, *Zorba the Greek,* trans. Carl Wildman (New York: Ballantine Books, 1964), p. 334.

6. *Cherry-Blossoms: Japanese Haiku,* Series III (Mt. Vernon, N.Y.: Peter Pauper Press, 1960), p. 55.

7. Frederic Spiegelberg, *Zen, Rocks, and Waters,* intro. Herbert Read (New York: Pantheon Books, 1961), plate V.

8. *Wind Bell* 14, no. 1 (Summer 1975): 16. See also 9, nos. 3–4 (Fall–Winter 1970–71), and other issues.

9. Jan Fontein and Money L. Hickman, eds. *Zen Painting and Calligraphy* (Boston: Museum of Fine Arts, 1970), pp. 52–53.

10. Harold G. Henderson, commentary and trans., *An Introduction to Haiku: An Anthology of Poems from Basho to Shiki* (Garden City: Doubleday, 1958), p. 133.

11. *Wind Bell* 9, nos. 3–4 (Fall–Winter 1970–71): 46.

12. Lucien Stryk and Ikemoto Takahashi, trans. and eds., *Zen Poems, Prayers, Sermons, Anecdotes, Interviews* (Garden City: Doubleday, 1965), p. 16.

13. Abe Masao, " 'Life and Death' and 'Good and Evil' in Zen," *Criterion* (Autumn 1969): 5. Undergirds much of this section.

14. Shibayama Zenkei, *Zen Comments on the Mumonkan,* trans. Kudo Sumiko, pref. Kenneth W. Morgan (New York: New American Library, 1974), p. 329.

15. *Cherry Blossoms,* p. 49.

16. *Cherry Blossoms,* p. 52.

17. Eihei-ji publication (Eihei-ji-cho, Yoshida-gun, Fukui-ken, Japan, n. d.), p. 7. My trans., my itals.

18. William F. Kraft, *A Psychology of Nothingness* (Philadelphia: Westminster Press, 1974), pp. 145–46. Also Stanley Keleman, *Living Your Dying* (New York: Random House, 1974).

19. *Cherry Blossoms,* p. 61.

20. Harold Stewart, essay and trans., *A Net of Fireflies: Japanese Haiku and Haiku Paintings* (Tokyo: Charles E. Tuttle, 1960), p. 155.

21. Abe, " 'Life and Death,' " p. 2.

22. Lin Yutang, trans. and ed., *The Importance of Understanding: Translations from the Chinese* (Cleveland: World Publishing, 1960), p. 462.

23. Philip Kapleau, *The Three Pillars of Zen* (New York: Harper & Row, 1969), p. 200.

Four

CHRISTIANITY AND ZEN-
ALIKE AND UNLIKE

One minute of sitting, one inch of Buddha.
Like lightning all thoughts come and pass.
Just once look into your mind-depths:
Nothing else has ever been.

Tokuo

God has revealed to us through the Spirit.
For the Spirit searches everything, even the
depths of God. For who knows a person's
    thoughts
except the spirit of the person which is inside?

1 Cor. 2:10–11

Comparisons

On the surface of a lotus pond there are many leaves and blossoms, different and identifiable because of color and shape. The leaves and blossoms are all joined by their stems to one tap root, deep in the bottom of the pond. The figure of the lotus pond, so often used by Buddhists, speaks about difference and sameness and about the ancient problem of the many and the one. The lotus pond is also an analogy for thinking about the religions of the world. There are uniquenesses and contrasts in religions, as seen in their practices, beliefs, and perspectives, but at the bottom they are joined because of common declarations and assumptions. All religions are concerned with some quality of life, such as love or compassion; some concept of ultimate reality; some sense of connection with this reality, whether known in faith, adoration, obedience, or an undefined responsiveness; some type of ritual; and some form of human responsibility. The tap root of all religions offers the possibility of dialogue and mutual understanding.

But the tap root does not tell us much about the vibrancy of religions or about their real nature and function. The common declarations and assumptions are general. Too much can be claimed for them. Each chapter of this book begins with a Zen saying or poem and a biblical passage; the two quotations seem to be saying much the same thing and therefore appear to be part of the tap root in the lotus pond. But I view them as having more connection with the surface. They are offered as a kind of mondo, a succinct, probing statement, providing an incentive to question the words and to discover what is really being said. Despite the parallel language and the connection between the ideas presented, the content of the opening Zen and the biblical lines is different. They belong on the top of the pond, displaying difference and contrast. In this sense, they are true-to-life sayings, for most of us are aware of and look for specificity and uniqueness in our quest for religious perspective. We live on the surface. It is a Zen point that unity and connection arise out of our experience of difference and contrast.

One of the problems in claiming too much for the tap root or commonality of religions is that one religion can so easily be merged and even identified with another. Difference is forgotten in the search for similarity and shared ground; one religion is often presented in the guise of another. There cannot be, I believe, any Christianizing of

Hakuin's painting of Bodhidharma or Daruma.
The calligraphy reads:
"Pointing directly to your own heart:
See your own nature and become Buddha."

Courtesy of a private collection, New Orleans, Louisiana.

Zen or "Zenifying" of Christianity. Despite claims by some that the two have similar methods and goals—that Christian meditation and prayer, for example, resemble zazen—my experience has led me to see sharp contrast.

The United Church of Christ church to which my family and I belong and where I have served as interim minister once held a "meditation" within the confines of the regular Sunday morning public worship. As we sat in our pews, row upon row with latched doors on the aisles, we were asked at the beginning of the service to be quiet and then to read to ourselves these words:

> I am here.
> Let me be wholly here.
> What sounds do I hear, loud and quiet, near and far,
>   without and within . . .
> I am here, now.
> I clear my mind of regrets, old angers, obligations,
>   unfinished plans,
> Of worries, fears, anxieties, hopes. I drop them
>   into the hands of God beneath me.
> I am clear; here, now, listening.
> I am here in the presence of God . . . .
> Praise the Lord, O my soul: All that is
>   within me, bless His name.
> Amen.

The experience was presented as a Christian example of Eastern meditation. I found that I was uncomfortable for two reasons. First, the meditation seemed out of place as a prelude to the readings, sermon, hymns, prayers of our public worship service. A time of undirected silence might have been more effective. Second, despite claims of similarity to Zen, I discovered very few, if any, parallels to zazen. Not only were we shut in pews, symbolically cutting ourselves off from other people and other things, but we concentrated on words; we spoke about being in the presence of God; and we blessed the name of the Lord. Absent was the zazen stress on connection with each other, whether facing the wall or facing each other, all joined by the emptiness in the middle, and gone was the Zen insistence on "no words" and body centering. The presence and fullness of a saving God was stressed, not the emptying of self and discovery of wholeness within.

My approach is to concentrate on the differences—even the opposite natures—of Zen and Christianity while exploring some connections they have in the tap root. I do this on the basis of my Zen experience in meditation, esthetics, mind-body training, art, and humor. My background in Christianity also argues for stressing differences. I speak out of the Reformed heritage which asserts that the Puritans and Jonathan Edwards still have much to say about the importance of the covenant of grace and human responsiveness. My theological perspectives are also rooted in the thought of such modern figures as H. Richard Niebuhr, Paul Tillich, and Thomas J. J. Altizer.

Those who see great parallels between Zen and Christianity and even a possibility of combining practices and perspectives stand in the Roman Catholic tradition. Heinrich Dumoulin, Dom Aelred Graham, William Johnston, H. M. Enomiya Lassalle, Thomas Merton—each an authoritative and imaginative presenter of Zen to the Western world—see a profound association. William Johnston, friend and fellow participant in zazen at Myoshin-ji in Kyoto, perhaps states the case best of all in his book *Christian Zen.* Many lines of connection are established between the two traditions, for example, the use of paradox, meditative practices, the sense of ritual. However, the strongest parallel between Zen and Christianity can be drawn, it is asserted, because of the mystical tendency of each. Such authors find that the medieval Rhineland devotionalists, the anonymous author of the *Cloud of Unknowing*, Saint John of the Cross, and the Hesychasts who practice breath concentration during contemplation have much in common with Eisai, Dogen, and Hakuin. Such Eastern and Western figures share a distrust of reasoning, an insistence on "seeing directly" into the cause and meaning of phenomena, and a belief in meditation as a way of understanding unity and reality. Teilhard de Chardin is often cited as a modern example of such a link between Christianity and Zen. However, these and other Christian mystics speak, in the end, of union with God and a vision of the cosmic Christ, who, as the eternal Word, is coextensive with the universe. Zen Buddhism has no such final referents.

A major question is to be considered in the tracing of such parallelism: How mystical is Zen? To be sure, there are "flights of the soul," an entrance into another dimension, the jolting and instructive use of paradox, and an emphasis on "seeing into." But Zen is not otherworldly. It does not point toward a union with something transcendent. Zen has a historical connection with the samurai, the warrior or swordsman class in Japan; it stresses a "return to the market place" in the ox-herding paintings and captions; its discipline is aimed at bringing one down from the isolation of the mountain peak to the involvement of the valley. Zen always speaks of function and wholeness in the everyday world. Although associated in part with mysticism, Zen has greater connection with Max Weber's religious and sociological classification known as "inner-worldly asceticism."

There is always some connection between Christianity and Zen, as there is between all perspectives known as religious. Shibayama Zenkei tells a story about Ryokan (1757–1831), the Japanese Zen poet, artist, and comic spirit. On an autumn evening lit by a bright moon, Ryokan came back to his hermitage to find that his belongings—few in number, but all that he possessed—had been stolen. "He then made a haiku poem:

> The moon out the window!
> Left by the thief unstolen.

Does he not somehow resemble Saint Francis of Assisi?"[1] A delightful and true connection! Each did live in a spirit of unattachment and spontaneity. But Shibayama does not go on to claim deep parallelism in the thought and spiritual discipline of Ryokan and Francis. What meaningful similarity is there between Ryokan's major pursuit of playing the divine fool and cavorting with village children and Francis's supreme devotion to the dying figure of Jesus on the cross and finally receiving the stigmata?

It is sometimes said that Jesus' sayings resemble those of a Zen master. No doubt similarities flash across the mind. Alan Watts calls attention to the freedom and the precariousness which both Jesus and many Zen figures portray about themselves. A Zen saying is:

> Above, not a tile to cover the head;
> Below, not an inch of ground for the foot.

How close this brushes to Jesus' words about himself: "Foxes have holes, and birds of the air have nests; but the Son of man has nowhere to lay his head (Luke 9:58)."[2]

Jesus' parables and directives often have a Zen ring when one listens closely to their short cadence, abruptness, directness, and paradox. He tells us in the Gospels to let the dead bury the dead; he urges us in a seeming turn-about to render to Caesar the things that are Caesar's; and he refuses to explain the basis of forgiving the adulterous woman, writing cryptically in the sand. Perhaps he sounds like a Zen master most of all when he states with enigmatic force: "Truly, truly, I say to you, before Abraham was, I am (John 8:58)." A koan often given by masters is: "What was your original face before your parents were born!" or "See yourself before you were born!" Over and again, Jesus speaks of the importance of the moment, of making decisions now, or finding the kingdom where one is and not simply waiting for the great time that is to come. The sign or message of the prophet Jonah, which Jesus gave his listeners, is to repent now and make amends so that life may be lived fully (Matt. 12:38–42).

But the divergence is pronounced. Few would be content to call Jesus a Zen master and search for his identity in the fleeting similarities. Jesus does stress the moment, but he also teaches preparation for the end, or a future time of righteousness. The pronounced social concern of Jesus is not directly shared by Zen. One parable tells us, "For behold, the kingdom of God is within you (Luke 17:21)"; but Jesus is not urging the "inward looking" of Zen, not saying that all things can be found inside, and not indicating that God-centeredness (like Buddha nature) is to be found in ourselves. The Greek and the Aramaic in this saying might better be translated to say that the kingdom is "available to us," or better, "among us." Men and women have a responsibility for the full sense of justice in society—taking part in the bringing in of this justice is to enter the kingdom.

Saint Paul writes that Jesus "emptied himself (Phil. 2:7)." But this is not a Zen emptying whereby one lets all thoughts, forms, desires, aspirations fall away in the discipline of zazen or in mind-body training, so that one may enter a "place" of connection and unity. It is rather an emptying so that the form of a servant, even a suffering servant, willing to submit to death on a cross, might be assumed.

Fragmentary similarities and crossings there may be between Zen teachers and Jesus and other New Testament figures. But the way of Zen is not the way of the cross. The perspective which, on the one hand, views Buddha as Tathagata, "the one who has come through," and that which, on the other, views Jesus as suffering Lord and Word of God are different in form and substance.

Fascinating correspondences between Zen and Christianity continue throughout their histories. Whereas Roman Catholic colleagues in Zen studies point to parallels between Christianity and Zen in the medieval Western mystics, I would call attention to overlooked similarities which occur in the Puritan tradition. I speak of the early Puritan theologians and statesmen active in England and in America from about 1575 to 1650—men such as William Ames (1576–1633), Thomas Cartwright (1535–1603), John Cotton (1584–1652), Thomas Hooker (1586?– 1647), William Perkins (1558–1602), Richard Sibbes (1577–1635), John Winthrop (1588–1649). The Puritan insistence on simplicity in worship and ecclesiastical organization compares with Zen procedures and standards for sittings and services. More important, out of a common concern for simplicity come parallels relating to use of words and to *praxis,* or religious discipline.

William Ames may stand as a representative of the English-American group, although variations and differences existed among members. Ames's personal stature and his writings cast a predominant influence on many in the Old and New Worlds of the seventeenth and eighteenth centuries, including Jonathan Edwards. His works were still required reading for American students in philosophy and "divinity" at the time of the Revolution. Ames and his fellow Puritans could and did preach long sermons, but they also believed that a theologian's ideas could and should be put forward in a pithy, brief "compendium." One of Ames's most important works, which had nineteen printings, was entitled *The Marrow of Theology*. The book was written in the early seventeenth century when Ames was in exile in the Netherlands; the language was Renaissance Latin, an advantage which gave the text the possibility of being taken up by anyone with a rudimentary education in the 1600's, whether the reader was English, French, Dutch, or German. In the "Brief Forewarning" of the book, Ames states: "When language flows on in a swift stream, carrying with it many things of many kinds, the reader can catch and hold fast to very little. He cannot find a resting place." At the end of the two-page preface, he writes: "And I confess that I share that heresy which bids me, when teaching, not to say in two words what may be said in one and which allows me to choose the key which best opens the lock. The key may well be made of wood, if the golden key does not work."

In the *Marrow*, Ames urges his readers to focus their thought and scriptural meditation on a few single points, rather than sweep with their mind's eye over a large intellectual and spiritual landscape. The concentration of which he speaks is like the focusing urged by a Zen master, who might speak about "going into" a particular koan, or about the most effective *mudra*, position of the hands, or about counting breaths. "A contracted light, although it may appear small, is more enlightening (if a man comes near and observes) than one which is, as it were, dissipated by two much enlargement."[3] Throughout, the *Marrow* has Zen directness, sparseness, and intensity.

Neither Puritanism nor Zen have pronounced metaphysical concerns. Rather, each movement puts great emphasis on the living of a religious perspective. Both have a suspicion of theory and urge their followers to see the religious way as more than an exercise of the mind. To be sure, Puritan theologians were among the intellectual giants of the day at Cambridge University, Harvard College, and Dutch universities, as were (and are) Zen teachers at Japanese temples, schools, and educational institutions. But the person who lives in the covenant of grace or who lives in *samadhi*, the ongoing sense of interconnection and unity, is not the person who only resides in the bliss of thought and conceptualization. For the Puritans, the good life is known by its ability to accept God's initiative in the covenant of grace; one's life is to be an actual response to God's calling in the covenant. For Zen teachers, it is not important—in fact, it could be detrimental—to dwell on the meaning of enlightenment or of *sunyata*, emptiness. Dogen said over and again to his followers, "Practice is enlightenment."

As the Puritan considers his major task to be that of living out his thankfulness for being in the covenant of grace, so the Zen person lives out in meditation and compassion his thanksgiving for the teaching and direction of Buddha and the patriarchs. Ames, speaking for all Puritans, writes in the very beginning of the *Marrow*, "Theology is the teaching of living to God." And Dogen in the *Shusho-gi, Discourse on the Training of Enlightenment*, says, "The true way of expressing this gratitude is not to be found in anything other than our daily Buddhist practice—selflessly esteeming each day of life."[4]

The how and the way of being religious are always at the

fore in Puritanism and Zen. William Ames, following the lead of earlier English Puritans, placed a chart or "method" at the beginning of *The Marrow of Theology.* The chart explains the meaning of theology in outline form, bracketing subtopics together in couplets. The "method," spreading over several pages, looks like a tennis-tournament chart in reverse. Theology is divided into two main parts: faith in God and "observance." The second part, concerned with Puritan practice, is typical of the movement's emphasis; it deals with the proper form of worship, the heeding of the psalmist's advice to seek God early in the morning, the meaning of loving one's neighbor, the kinds of prayer. Zen masters have similar directives or methods about the details of sitting, about life together in the temple community, and about compassionate acts in the world beyond the temple.

Zen and Puritanism both urge their practitioners to be more than they think themselves to be. Reassurance is offered to those who want to enter the full dimension of each way. A favorite text of Puritan preachers is "Seek first his kingdom and his righteousness (Matt. 6:33)." Act as if you were in the covenant of grace and believe that you are—aim high, even though you are aware of shortcomings and continue to examine your spiritual condition. A Zen saying, relating to questions and fears about discipline, is: "If you want to climb a mountain, begin at the top." Believe that you can find a good "place," even at the very beginning; depend on the teaching of the tradition and on your concentration and perseverance. This hopeful beginner's mind is always Zen mind, as Suzuki Shunryu reminds us in *Zen Mind, Beginner's Mind.*

Lastly, the new kind of logic used by the Puritans of the late sixteenth and early seventeenth centuries has great similarity to the koan practice of Zen. English and American Puritans, particularly those educated at Cambridge University, adopted a form of logic and reasoning which departed from traditional Aristotelianism. Ramist logic, named after Peter Ramus, who perished at the height of his powers in the Saint Bartholomew's Day massacre in Paris in 1572, broke away from reasoning which depended on syllogism and assignment to categories. According to Ramus, when one is faced with a problem or a decision, one is to ask a question about the matter, then divide the question into its two major parts, and finally "invent" or discover a "middle term" or "argument" which will provide an answer or understanding by relating the two parts of the question. The Puritans used Ramist logic in their analysis and interpretation of the Bible, rather than amass key texts and syllogistic proofs, as other Reformed theologians had done. When biblical syllogism was used by the Puritans, it had a personal, dialectical meaning and was not thought to be part of an objective verification process.

William Perkins, William Ames, and Thomas Hooker were among the chief adapters of Ramist logic to scriptural reasoning. Typical, perplexing, Puritan-Ramist questions, directed toward the Bible, might be: "How does God love us?" and "Do I have eternal life?" A diligent student of the scriptures is urged to find a middle term or argument (sometimes even an expression or an idea) in the Bible which would relate the parts of each question—"God" and "us" and "I" and "eternal life." In the first illustration, Puritan theologians often suggested, as one possibility, the general thesis of Paul's Letter to the Romans. In central passages in Romans, one could find a middle term which would join the "God" and "us" and provide at least a beginning answer to the question. In 5:8 Paul writes, "God shows his love for us in that while we were yet sinners Christ died for us." As one reflects on this passage as a possible middle term or connection, one could find a relationship between "God" and "us" and, hopefully, discover an answer to the "how" of God's love for us.

How does this kind of reasoning connect with koan practice—meditating on a probing, startling question given by a roshi and later "discussed" with him? Like a koan, Ramist logic functioned through a question, not a proposition or an assertion to be argued logically. Ramist-Puritan questions and Zen koan must be penetrating, possessing a "real life" dimension. Both involve wrestling and even agonizing—both are "paradigms of dislocation." If it were a genuine question in either tradition, it would not be solved easily. In many collections of koan, there were certain prescribed or traditional answers. But the existence of such a list and even the knowledge of its contents, did not guarantee an answer to the koan. Only when special insight was gained through meditation could an answer be "appropriated" and understood. The Puritans also had a list of possible answers, found in biblical sayings, themes, and arguments; the scriptures contained the Ramist "places" which would offer possible middle terms and thereby supply a beginning answer to the question. But, like Zen traditional answers, there was no easy assurance of understanding or solution unless one meditated on the scriptures and searched out the meaning of the biblical middle term.

The Puritans went beyond koan practice in the matter of personal discovery of an answer or an understanding. Not only were there standard places in the Bible which provided middle terms, such as the frequently cited main themes in the Letter to the Romans, but there were, considering all of scripture, places almost without limit. In the *Marrow,* Ames offers lavish biblical citations—not as proof texts, but as Ramist suggestions for middle terms. He seems to be saying to his readers, "Here is a possible connection between the parts of your question," or "Try this for a link." The Puritans urged those struggling with questions to find in the scriptures their own special middle terms which would provide answers. The Puritan theologians also urged followers, in distinction to Zen, to formulate their own questions, not just to accept those provided by a teacher.

But the differences are minor in the face of astounding similarities. Ramist logic and koan practice both stressed a spiritual struggle. Each method demanded that a person should become "lost" in the question proposed. Each urged trial and error as a method of discovering the connection or insight which, in the end, might work— conveying a common pragmatic concern. And Puritan and Zen agreed that genuine answers could not be supplied by an outside authority but must come through individual effort and discipline.

So Zen and Puritanism have these fascinating parallels, but what of their divergencies? Each has a root in the inner-worldly asceticism described by Max Weber. However, the root of one is Buddhist and the other is Christian; different trees of life and knowledge are produced. The christological emphasis in Puritanism has no counterpart in Zen Buddhism. The meditation commended by Puritan preachers is of a very different sort from the central practice of Zen. A Puritan believer is urged to meditate on the scriptures, especially on the middle term which relates to Ramist questions about salvation and eternal life. He is also urged to meditate on qualities of the Christian life; a typical Puritan list from Perkins, Ames, and Cotton might include love, humility, meekness, peace of conscience, and the glory of God's kingdom. In zazen, one is to let ideas about virtues and goals—and all thought—depart, so that one may hopefully reach a state of emptiness. Even in the case of the Puritan "mystics" (e.g., John Saltmarsh), the sense of reverie about God's love and mercy is vastly different from the purpose and method of zazen. Puritans understandably see God as the author and creator of their spiritual edification; there is to be no ultimate self-reliance, as in Zen. The Zen concern for the body and its association with mind and spiritual discipline are not found in Puritanism.

Both Puritanism and Zen uphold a close relationship and alternation between structure and antistructure. Each has its own set of prescriptions about the religious way— its own rituals and procedures. Each also stresses that controlling structure must at times be set aside. The Puritan is urged to find his own middle term in the scriptures in a way that often follows whimsy and individual choice. The Zen person is to work in solitude on the particular problems which plague his concentration. He will have to find his own path through the rigors of zazen—and the path will not be able to be charted for or even discussed with others.

But Zen far surpasses Puritanism in its use of antistructure. The *sumi-e,* brush and ink, painter will proceed through set lessons dealing with bamboo and winter sparrows, but then she is to depend on what she sees and inwardly understands as she draws. The person in zazen follows her mind's eye into emptiness—and each time she will take a different route. The observer of a beautiful object has no rules to follow as she lets the object enter her consciousness—except that she try to impose no structure on what is before her. The aikido trainee cannot predict how the *ki,* or universal energy, will enter her body and movements, nor can she control or structure the relationship between herself and cosmic force. The honoring of the structurelessness of events and conditions and the attendant stress on Taoist *wei wu wei,* doing by not doing, are special Zen characteristics. They are found only in part among those on the Puritan way.

The discussion of parallelism between Christianity and Zen Buddhism might well continue, but I will mention only two other examples. The American Transcendentalists not only demonstrate similarities to Zen perceptions, but also were familiar with the Indian background of Zen. Ralph Waldo Emerson (1803–82) in his poem "Brahma" and elsewhere spoke about the relationship of opposites in a Buddhist way. His concept of the "oversoul" has some parallels to the Zen understanding of unity and connection. On the way from Concord to Cambridge to deliver his "Divinity School Address" he observed with a Zen eye the summer fields refulgent in sunshine and hues and remarked about them at the beginning of his speech. But Emerson knew little, if anything, about *sunyata,* or emptiness, and did not advocate a discipline of meditation or an esthetic understanding parallel to that of Zen. Henry David Thoreau (1817–62) exceeded Emerson in his power to observe and to portray natural objects. He developed beside Walden Pond and elsewhere his own kind of meditation, which had similiarites to zazen; Thoreau insisted that one was not to impose meaning and conditions upon objects but to take them into consciousness as they were. He spoke of individuality and uniqueness in a style and content reminiscent of Zen masters. "Why should not we have a poetry and philosophy of insight and not of tradition, a religion by revelation to us, and not the history of theirs?"[5] Although one of the thinkers in American intellectual history close to Zen, Thoreau was also distant. His ideas on the power of literary symbolism and imagination would have little meaning to a Zen Buddhist. His conception of reality had greater connection with Indian Hindu concepts of *Brahman,* the primordial, given unity from which all things come. He did not see unity arising out of the dynamics of relationship between the particulars of, say, Zen "blue mountain" and "white cloud." Ultimate unity was postulated by Thoreau, and all things were assumed to have a connection with an abiding, elemental level of being and reality.

In more recent times, parallels could be cited between Zen and the "process theologians," those developing creatively—and also departing from—the work of Alfred North Whitehead. Charles Hartshorne, Schubert M. Ogden, John B. Cobb, Jr., Bernard E. Meland, and others have strong leanings toward forms of Zen Buddhist understanding. The Whiteheadian point that every "trivial puff of existence" has reality is not far from the assertion of the Buddhahood of all things. Process theology has other associations with Zen: the newness and continual development of human experience, the insistence on concrete immediacy in perception, a concern for a connected pluralistic universe, the interest in "becoming" as opposed to being. But process theologians are nonetheless Christian theologians who speak of transcendent God (although in new ways), of the saving power of the divine Logos, and of the power of words and intellective understanding.

So parallels between Zen and Christianity are present, but they do not run deep. They are of interest and often of fascination and surprise, but they are to be seen against the broad perspectives of each tradition. Nishida may speak of God in a *Study of Good,* but he is not speaking of the Christian god who has transcendent qualities and to whom the role of creation is assigned. Rather, God is a manifestation of the unity found in the interaction of all things and qualities in the world. Nishida speaks of God as the relationship between essence and phenomenon. Christians would say more. Not only is God involved in creation, but also in the meaning of love and the sense of the ending.

A case in point

In the 1740s, two men, one Japanese and the other colonial American, reached the height of their powers as religious teachers and thinkers. Each lived and worked in communities removed from centers of cultural and educational fame. The first had returned to his birthplace, to the small village of Hara, near the foot of Mount Fuji—a good journey from Edo, later called Tokyo, and a longer journey from Kyoto. The other lived in Northampton, almost the frontier of the Massachusetts Bay Colony, in the Connecticut River Valley—a good journey from either Boston or New York. Each had returned "home" for his major work. The Zen teacher and master came back to Shoin-ji, a temple surrounded by a pine grove, which had no resident priest and was in a state of disrepair. Shoin-ji under his leadership was to become the center of the most influential Buddhist revival in the Tokugawa period. The theologian and scholar settled as minister in the Church of Northampton, where his grandfather, Solomon Stoddard, had served for many years. The Northampton church had once been the center of many spiritual "harvests," but now a listlessness and dullness prevailed. This church was soon to become a place where, through his preaching and ministry, a new movement and spirit would arise.

Hakuin Ekaku (1685–1768) became known as "the greatest sage in five hundred years" and the "patriarch who revived Zen." Disciples flocked around him at mid-century, as they did until his death; his annual public lectures drew hundreds of students and Zen followers; he wrote poetry, commentaries, and tracts; he left behind paintings of delicacy and great spiritual meaning, dealing with Zen figures and topics. Jonathan Edwards (1703–58), often considered to be America's most influential theologian, was the preacher and moving force in the Great Awakening of the 1730s and 1740s. Edwards's mind was so far-ranging and imaginative that the full circle of his thought includes religious philosophy, pastoral theology, biblical exegesis, and a brilliant combination of Reformed doctrine and Enlightenment insight.

In the 1740s, both Hakuin and Edwards were working on summary statements of their religious perceptions and beliefs. Hakuin was composing a moving and penetrating poem known as *Zazen Wasan,* or the "Song of Zazen." Jonathan Edwards was preaching sermons which were to become in 1746 a major work known as a *Treatise Concerning Religious Affections.* These two contemporaries and these two works stand as a revealing case in point for the relationship of Zen and Christianity. They also stand as influential representatives of Zen and Christianity in me.

Hakuin wrote the "Song of Zazen" not only to praise and magnify the central practice of Zen. The poem's aim is to present the true nation of religious experience and perception, to indicate the line between true and false practice, and to offer encouragement to Zen practitioners. The "Song" is only forty-four lines; it is thought to be a gem of summary and inspiration, offering sparse and penetrating insight into such terms as Buddhahood and *samadhi,* the sense of union or connection. Throughout the Mahayana world, the poem has been widely read, meditated upon, and chanted. A portion of the "Song of Zazen" reads:

> All beings are primarily Buddhas.
> Like water and ice,
> There is no ice apart from water;
> There are no Buddhas apart from beings.

Jonathan Edwards—American theologian,
leader of the Great Awakening,
and preacher of "religious affections."

Portrait by Joseph Badger. Courtesy of Yale University.

Not knowing how close the Truth is to them,
Beings seek for it afar—what is pity!
It is like those who being in water
Cry out for water, feeling thirst . . .

As to Zazen taught in the Mahayana,
No amount of praise can exhaust its merits . . .

But if you turn your eyes within yourselves
And testify to the truth of Self-nature—
The Self-nature that is no nature,
You will have gone beyond the ken of sophistry.

The gate of the oneness of cause and effect
    is opened;
The path of nonduality and nontrinity
    runs straight ahead.
Your form being the form of no form,
Your going-and-returning takes place
    nowhere but where you are . . .

How boundless and free is the sky of *Samadhi!*
How refreshingly bright, the moon of the
    Fourfold Wisdom!
At this moment what is there that you lack!
Nirvana presents itself before you,
Where you stand is the Land of Purity.
Your person, the body of Buddha.[6]

Jonathan Edwards wrote the *Religious Affections* with a similar purpose in mind. In the midst of the bitter controversy over the Great Awakening, Edwards noted the "lifelessness" of prevailing religion; yet he denounced those who depended solely on emotional responses as a sign of faith. "Gracious affections do arise in the mind's being enlightened, rightly and spiritually to understand or apprehend divine things. Holy affections are not heat without light." [7] The true nature of religion inevitably involves a blend of mind and heart. And, like Hakuin in the "Song," Edwards always spoke a word of exhortation and support to his hearers. Edwards inherited Puritan longevity as well as directness—he could speak and write succinctly, but the forty-four lines of the "Song" would have been out of the question! He presented the collected sermons in three major parts, concluding with a discussion of the twelve signs of "truly gracious and holy affections." Although long and involved, the *Religious Affections* is not a collection of cold, analytic arguments and theses. The very issues and happenstances under discussion are presented so artfully that they lure a hearer or a reader—even a late-twentieth-century one—into the matters at hand.

> There is no question whatsoever, that is of greater importance to mankind, and that it more concerns every individual person to be well resolved in, than this, what are the distinguishing qualifications of those that are in favor with God, and entitled to his eternal rewards. . . . So has God disposed things, in the affair of our redemption, and in his glorious dispensations, revelaed to us in the Gospel, as though everything were purposely contrived in such a manner, as to have the greatest, possible tendency to reach our hearts in the most tender part, and move our affections most sensibly and strongly. . . . Those affections that are truly holy, are primarily founded on the moral excellency of divine things. Or (to express it otherwise) a love to divine things for the beauty and sweetness of their moral excellency, is a first beginning and spring of all holy affections. . . . A true love to God must begin with a delight in his holiness, and not with a delight in any other attribute; for no other attribute is truly lovely without this, and

no otherwise than as . . . it derives its loveliness from
this; and therefore it is impossible that other attributes should appear lovely, in their true loveliness,
till this is seen.[8]

What shall we say about these two eighteenth-century
contemporaries who lived cultures apart—and a continent
and an ocean apart? Hakuin, who lived gracefully into his
old age, and Edwards, cut off rudely at his prime by a
smallpox epidemic. These two who never knew each
other, but who are joined together in others' favorable
judgment about contribution to their traditions. These
two, each possessed of an austere, perhaps removed,
spirit—whose unavoidable eyes, set in oval faces, con-
veyed both intensity and understanding. Hakuin, known
as one who could do zazen hour upon hour almost without
end, and who languished with the "Zen sickness" of
fatigue and malnutrition. And Edwards, who normally
spent twelve hours a day in study and in writing and who,
when walking the streets of Northampton and later the
pathways of Stockbridge, appeared lost in deep contemplation. Hakuin and Edwards, each so perceptive, so artful,
so brilliant, and so concentrated.

Both the "Song" and the *Religious Affections* are works of
power because of their artistry. As Hakuin praises zazen,
the lines flow together almost as if they were connected
haiku. The one who seeks truth far away is "like the rich
man's son who has lost his way among the poor." And on
the new spirit possible in Zen he declares, "How refreshingly bright, the moon of the Fourfold Wisdom!" Indeed,
it is said of Hakuin that even his most ordinary discourses
to his followers and members of the Shoin-ji community
were spoken in linked verse. As for Edwards, a reader
admires not only his logic and clarity, but his special way

with words. His use of positive, warming expressions to speak of a person's "closing with Christ" in the *Religious Affections* and other works has an illuminative and vivid quality. "Taste and see; never was any disappointed that made a trial. You will not only find those spiritual comforts that Christ offers you to be of a surpassing sweetness for the present, but they will be to your soul as the dawning light that shines more and more to the perfect day; and the issue of all will be your arrival in heaven." [9] As Hakuin took brush in hand and presented anecdotes of Zen patriarchs and Zen ideas of function and simplicity on rice paper, so Jonathan Edwards was an artist of the mind, who spoke effectively about space, light, seeing, color, and taste.

Edwards and Hakuin honored the tradition out of which they had come, but each can rightly be called an innovator. Jonathan Edwards spoke about the idea of a "new sense" or a "new simple idea" in religious conviction. People might have listened before to the gospel being preached and might have admitted in their mind its force, but now, Edwards urged, people should find and develop an ability to "see" and feel the gospel's truth. The "sense of the heart" is over and again discussed in the *Affections*. Believers must not only study and think, but they must listen to the reasons of the heart. The "new sense" involves a direct, overwhelming apprehension of the gospel, using all of one's sensory and intellectual capacities. Hakuin, as a Zen teacher, naturally spoke about the function of the total self, whether one heeded the Soto stress on zazen or the Rinzai stress on meditation and koan. He urged his practitioners to be experimenters, perhaps more so than any other Zen master. Instead of using only standard collections of koans, Hakuin often invented new ones for his students. His most famous is, "What is the sound of one hand clapping?" (Hakuin so inspired a Japanese-American friend of mine that he also offered a new koan: "What is the sound of one lip whistling?" Hakuin would have liked that!)

The list of parallels could go on and on. Both Hakuin and Edwards believed in and spoke incessantly about religious discipline and training. In the classic Zen doctrine of egolessness, Hakuin, like Dogen, urged the forgetting of self in the simple unfolding of practice. Jonathan Edwards preached over and again about self-effacement and self-denial before God. "Be not wise in your own eyes; fear the Lord (Prov. 3:72)." Hakuin and Edwards believed that the significance of the religious life had an immediate meaning and chance of fulfillment. One did not have to go through the rounds of transmigration in order to be fully enlightened, according to Hakuin. And Edwards, like the Puritans, spoke always about the possibility of entering immediately into the fullness of the covenant of grace. True affections can operate now and need not wait for a better time or a coming kingdom. And for each there was to be continuing discipline after enlightenment and conversion. Hakuin insisted on post-enlightenment training as one of the levels of spiritual growth. Jonathan Edwards in his discussion of sanctification spoke of a perpetual examination of the heart and a continual inquiry of the interior spirit to see whether it be of God.

The disciplined religious way, for both Hakuin and Edwards, did not consist of life-denying rigor and practice. Each sitting, according to Hakuin, was unique and had its own special role to play in the quest for true mind. Every zazen enriched the participant in some way. Likewise, Edwards believed that the serious dealing with ideas, the diligent study of the scriptures, the preaching and hearing of the word were "renewing" and "sweet to the taste." Edwards stated that Christian discipline inexplicably effects a new sense, creates eyes to see and ears to hear, and turns darkness into light. As the rule of the contemporary Taizé Community says, in an Edwardsean phrase, "In the regularity of the office, the love of Jesus springs up, we know not how." Zen and Christian discipline and structure produce newness, enabling power, and freshening.

Lastly, both Hakuin and Edwards make imaginative uses of nature in the development of their perspectives. Hakuin often spoke about Mount Fuji, living as he did for most of his mature life in the shadow of this symbol of Japan. Rising over his village and surroundings, Fuji-san became, as is so often the case with Zen people about mountains, a thing of beauty, "suchness," and revealing power. He once wrote, "My sweetheart is dear Fuji, sitting on the clouds. How I long to see her snow white skin!"[10] The meaning of the words is not exhausted in the sensual reference; rather, the lines are to be understood as a statement about "true mind." Fuji-san is often hidden by clouds; but, when the weather is clear, it looms over the plain—massively and majestically. In order to see Fuji clearly, the clouds must go away. In order to find true mind, the clouds of dualism, prejudgment, and words must be removed. Jonathan Edwards, writing about the "beauty of holiness" in the *Affections* and elsewhere, used references to the world of nature over and again. He sounded every bit a Zen master when he wrote these words about immobility and seeing: "I often used to sit and view the moon for continuance." When one lives in the new sense of the affections and observes clouds, trees, the sun, and blue sky, one can see God's excellency, wisdom, and other attributes. God can also be discovered in the first clap of a thunderstorm.[11]

So, there are fascinating parallels between the dedicated, inspirational reviver of Zen in the plain of Mount Fuji and the brilliant, moving preacher-theologian of the Connecticut Valley. But Hakuin and Jonathan Edwards went, in the end, along divergent paths and offered their students, hearers, and readers different interpretations of the human situation.

As physicians of the soul, Hakuin and Edwards saw dissimilar basic predicaments of life. The *Affections* and other writings are full of references to human sin, which, according to Edwards's traditional interpretation, separates women and men from God, prevents exercise of the true affections, and produces a feeling and conviction of guilt. We must, at all times, know "the truth of what the Scripture reveals concerning the corruption of man's nature, his original sin, and the ruinous undone condition man is in, and his need of a Saviour, his need of the mighty power of God to renew his heart and change his nature." [12]

For Hakuin, there may be aspects of human life that keep people from seeing their true mind—as the clouds so often encircle Fuji-san and prevent a clear vision of its symmetry and white-capped summit. But these impairments are the result of human ignorance, known in dualistic thinking, lack of practice, and dependence on intellectual distinctions. The failings which Hakuin identifies are those which have grown out of incorrect teaching, unexamined habits, and a refusal to "see the nature of things directly." These defects are not to be compared with Edwards's notion of an original and inherited sin which describes the very condition of human existence, which has a willful and pernicious quality, and for which lamentation must continually be made. Hakuin, following traditional, sanguine Zen ways, does not concentrate on the things that separate people from the *dharma,* or true reality. Whatever the defects of life are, discipline and practice can overcome them. Even a single sitting can "erase the countless sins" of one's past.

The prescriptions and remedies of the two physicians differ radically also. For Hakuin, a person must discover what he already has inside. "Turn your eyes within yourselves and testify to the Truth of Self-nature," affirms the "Song of Zazen." Shibayama Zenkei, commenting on the thought of Hakuin, tells a story of a medieval Zen master. "A monk asked Master Sanko one day, 'Please show me the essence of Zen.' Sanko at once replied and said, 'Look under your feet!' " The Zen quest for truth is not found far from ourselves—indeed, it is in our own mind, our own body, and under our feet.[13]

For Jonathan Edwards, on the other hand, the remedy for sin, the drawing close to God, the finding of gracious affections, the living in the covenant of grace—all goals of the Christian life—are possible because of the bestowal of God. Anything that comes solely from the inner recesses of one's being is suspect. "The nature of the covenant of grace, and God's declared ends in the appointment and constitution of things in that covenant, do plainly show it to be God's design to make ample provision . . . . For so are all things ordered and contrived in that covenant, that everything might be made sure on God's part. The covenant is ordered in all things and sure: the promises are most full."[14]

So reliant was Hakuin upon the self and its resources, that Edwards most surely would have called him a victim of Arminianism—that which he and earlier Puritans hated most! Edwards, following William Ames and John Cotton, waged a lifelong battle against this often-maligned school, which urged, among other things, that salvation depended upon the action of the self and that good works could produce a closeness to God.

For Hakuin there is radical self-dependence, and for Edwards there must be God dependence. It is the difference, as Japanese would say, between *jiriki,* self power, and *tariki,* other power. Hakuin urges us to look inside, because we have been born with the power of discovering our Buddhahood. Edwards urges us to look beyond ourselves and to accept conversion by God's power to new perspectives and truth. For Hakuin, religious experience reveals a power that has always been within us; for Edwards, religious experience and the "religious affections" themselves are created and given by another power.

Jonathan Edwards also urges our dependence upon the Bible. Making less use of Ramist logic and thought than the Puritans, Edwards presents his ideas primarily as extended commentary on biblical texts. In his discussion of the "First Sign" in the *Affections,* for example, Edwards refers time and again to scriptural mention of the seals or marks which the saints possess. It is inconceivable that one could have true affections toward God or be in the covenant of grace without being dependent on the word of God in the Bible.

Hakuin knows the scriptures of his tradition well and urges his disciples to study them. But, in typical Zen spirit, he believes the sutras to be only small pinpoints of light, not to be compared with the full sunlight of the *dharma,* or ultimate reality. Study of scripture, dependence upon its doctrine, involvement in its argument could be entrapping. Hakuin endorses the ancient, simple Chinese phrases often used to describe Zen:

> Transmission outside scriptures,
> Not relying on letters,
> Pointing directly to one's Mind,
> Attainment of Buddhahood by seeing into one's Nature.

The forms of presentation used by Hakuin and Jonathan Edwards are vastly different. Edwards wrote the *Religious Affections* as a balanced treatise, weaving together his knowledge of John Locke's psychology and Isaac Newton's physics on the warp and woof of biblical ideas. The original sermons and the final statement were designed to persuade forcefully and to offer a "wisdom" about the place of emotion in religious life. Hakuin's "Song of Zazen" does not depend on reasoned discourse and careful phrases. The poem was written as praise for the discipline of sitting; it does not offer readers an opportunity to consider points of view. The work urges an elimination of discriminating consciousness and offers a way of grasping directly the unity of true mind. Edwards's *Affections* is a measured statement, subtly and forcefully presented; Hakuin's "Song" is a poetic confessional and an urging of a spiritual practice.

Jonathan Edwards believes that the culmination of time will take place in a future day of judgment. Although his concern with the end of the present age is not a primary interest in the *Affections,* it is an important consideration as he urges "professors" (those who speak openly of their convictions) to prepare for personal judgment, the end of time, and the beginning of eternity. In his "Farewell Sermon," delivered in Northampton in 1750 following a dispute with certain members of the congregation over qualifications for participation in Communion, Edwards spoke repeatedly about the reckoning at the end of time, "the day of infallible and of the unalterable sentence." [15]

Hakuin, true to the teachings of the Ch'an patriarchs and especially Dogen, folds the past and the future into the present. For one who truly practices zazen, the previous ages can be taken in and understood, and the future is looked at "directly" and entered. One who is living fully in the present has the mirror wisdom of Zen. The mirror reflects and takes in whatever comes before it. It can reflect the person standing before it, or the hallway from which a person has just come, or the passageway down which a person is going. Time markings coalesce in the distinction-lessness of practice. As Hakuin says in the "Song," "How boundless and free is the sky of *Samadhi!*"

Hakuin would not understand Jonathan Edwards's assertion that distinctions will be made among people on a day of judgment. Although there will be some who progress farther and more rapidly in practice than others, they are not to be viewed as having more merit or as occupying a special place—as are Edwards's "professors" of true religion. There is a consistent assertion in Hakuin of the spiritual worth of all people. A religious leader does not bemoan or threaten those who do not follow his teachings or those who hold a different theory of qualification for receiving the sacrament. Hakuin presents his Mahayana teaching forcefully, but passes no judgment on those who either reject or accept it. In the mid-eighteenth century, Hakuin was living out a contemporary Zen saying: "If a person knocks at the door, let him in; but if he leaves, do not pursue him."

As we have seen, both the *Affections* and the "Song" are full of references to nature, but they differ in their understanding of the meaning of natural beauty. Edwards's sense of beauty was unknown in his Puritan forebearers, who preferred rather to speak of nature as a "howling wilderness." Edwards's concern was part of his Enlightenment inheritance, which urged him to understand the whole world as a sure sign of balance and harmony. But Edwards was more concerned with the God who made the "fair proportion" than he was with the product. God as founding and maintaining power is the very source of beauty; the idea of God is the first and foremost matter of esthetics. Edwards often spoke about "giving consent." When one admires something that is beautiful, one gives consent not to the harmony and striking quality that is presented, but to the being that made such an object possible. To be attracted to beauty depends on the ability to give consent to being. Any signs of beauty, in the natural world or in Christian personal life, are to be admired and pursued in a secondary fashion. The primary reason for seeking them is because they are rooted in the nature and mind of God.[16]

Hakuin has, perhaps, an analogous framework, for all objects of beauty reflect, when one understands their relationship and ultimate unity, the Tao, the Way, or the *dharma,* abiding reality. But things can be beautiful by themselves in a primary fashion. As Taoists said centuries before, "The meaning of the beautiful is that which exists through itself." One can admire a beautiful tree for its symmetry, a cup of tea for its fragrance, and a mountain for its blueness without having a theory of unity or even a full understanding of the Tao or the *dharma.* Indeed, to have such theories prevents an understanding of the beautiful thing at hand. The theory comes out of the things themselves and is possible only because of the realities and particularities of the beautiful.

The natural objects which Edwards selects as affording an opportunity for consent to being are generally the grand and the dramatic. Among his favorites are sky, trees, storm clouds, and rainbows (but he is also very fond of spiders!). Hakuin's search for the beautiful leads him to the commonplace, the small, and the seemingly insignificant (but he is also very fond of mountains!). One of Hakuin's most famous paintings portrays an old bamboo broom whose worn stalks and well-rubbed handle have a charm and a sense of function which, along with the simple calligraphy, can only be called beautiful. Edwards, developing his sense of beauty, often looks up and about for his signs and examples. Hakuin looks down and around for his.

The preacher of the Great Awakening, although possessed of warmth and passion, was not a man of humor. The master of Shoin-ji, though a firm and disciplined teacher, was a person who believed in the comic, even the ridiculous. To be sure, stories are told about Edwards—about his losing his way home in Stockbridge while thinking about the next section of the *History of the Work of Redemption* and about his wry manner with people. A young man asked to marry Edwards's oldest daughter, Sarah, a woman of pronounced headstrong ways. Edwards, in all candor, spoke of her stubborness, even her temper. The young man still insisted and remarked, "But, Master Edwards, she has grace, has she not?" "Aye," said Edwards, "but grace can live where man cannot." Edwards's writings, however, never made use of humor as a way of instructing, of turning people aside to see something differently, or of creating a bond in a community, or of presenting an idea afresh. Hakuin, on the other hand, knew all these meanings of humor and used them in his teaching and writing. He even painted what might be called today cartoons. One of these paintings shows a one-eyed monster meeting a blind man. The monster is fierce and very ugly, with one large eye in the middle of his forehead. He glowers down at the blind man who is in his path and who raises up his head calmly and does not move. The colophon, or caption, of the painting reads: "Hey, I am a one-eyed monster. Aren't you afraid? Answer: Why should I be afraid of one eye? I have no eyes. It is you that should be scared of me."[17] It is a humorous painting and an arresting exchange of words in which the cutting down of the big and the fierce and the ascription of merit to inner strength are portrayed in a different way.

So Jonathan Edwards and Hakuin Ekaku understood many things alike, but a greater number of things differently. They represent a dramatic example of the relationship between Christianity and Zen Buddhism. And they stand for the connection of the two in me.

I have always been attracted to Edwards's sense of God's majesty and to his insistence on the place of meaningful "heart religion." He is a modern psalmist, who speaks about being filled with God, about the covenant of grace being "sweet to the taste," and about "pleasant places" wherein the spirit may be found. He is also a master of argument and expression. Edwards could analyze the religious affections without analyzing them away; all mystery is not dispelled. I warm to his interpretation of Puritan theology, a special field of interest to me, and in particular to his understanding and use of William Ames, a towering favorite figure of mine in the early seventeenth century. Jonathan Edwards—whose combination of scholarship, teaching, and preaching is a model for me in the late twentieth century, a model amazingly unblemished by eighteenth-century style and presentation. Jonathan Edwards—whose Connecticut Valley and Berkshire Hills I know well and call home.

Hakuin Ekaku is likewise a part of me. I am caught up in his perceptive mind, his simplicity, his practice, his directness, and his humor. He gives encouragement to all who know him, those who came to his temple during his lifetime and those who now read his works and view his paintings. I find association made easy because of the connection early in his life with Myoshin-ji in Kyoto, where I have engaged in Zen practice during three significant periods in my life. The spirit of Hakuin is especially close because I am a member of a community of Zen practitioners at Reiun-in, "Spirit of Cloud Temple," at Myoshin-ji. Hakuin—the realistic, gentle, demanding, compassionate master, whose influence on me is fresh and abiding.

Edwards and Hakuin do not stand for everything in Christianity and Zen Buddhism. But they do summarize many of the similarities and greater dissimilarities between the two perspectives. And, because of their excellence, Hakuin and Edwards provide many of the reasons why I journey between Zen and Christianity.

Notes

1. Shibayama Zenkei, *A Flower Does Not Talk* (Tokyo: Charles E. Tuttle, 1970), p. 137.
2. Alan W. Watts, *The Way of Zen* (N.Y.: Random House, 1957), p. x.
3. William Ames, *The Marrow of Theology*, trans., intro., ed. John D. Eusden (Philadelphia: United Church Press, 1968), pp. 69, 70. Erik F. Storlie, "Grace and Works, Enlightenment and Practice: Paradox and Poetry in John Cotton, Jonathan Edwards, and Dogen Zenji" (diss., University of Minnesota, 1976).
4. Yokoi Yuho, *Zen Master Dogen: An Introduction with Selected Writings*, with the assistance of Daizen Victoria (New York: Weatherhill, 1976), p. 63.
5. Henry D. Thoreau, *Walden*, ed. J. Lyndon Shanley (Princeton, N.J.: Princeton University Press, 1971).
6. Shibayama, *Flower*, pp. 65–67.
7. Jonathan Edwards, *Religious Affections*, intro. and ed., John E. Smith (New Haven: Yale University Press, 1959), p. 266.
8. Edwards, *Religious Affections*, pp. 84, 124, 253, 257.
9. Clarence H. Faust and Thomas H. Johnson, intro., notes, eds. *Jonathan Edwards: Representative Selections* (New York: Hill & Wang, 1962), p. cxii.
10. Shibayama, *Flower*, p. 74.
11. Faust and Johnson, *Jonathan Edwards*, p. cv.
12. Edwards, *Religious Affections*, p. 301.
13. Shibayama, *Flower*, pp. 128–29.
14. Edwards, *Religious Affections*, p. 169.

15. Faust and Johnson, *Jonathan Edwards*, p. 202.

16. Roland A. Delattre, *Beauty and Sensibility in the Thought of Edwards: An Essay in Aesthetics and Theological Ethics* (New Haven: Yale University Press, 1968), especially pp. 23, 25, 117.

17. Shibayama, *Flower*, p. 75.

Five

TWO WAYS TOGETHER

Stretched in the genial sun
The mountain snake
Tickled its length along the rock.
Takahashi

I was his delight day by day . . .
Playing on the surface of his earth
And I found delight in all people.
Prov. 8:30–31

Particularities and truth

Zen and Christian—alike, but more unlike. The particularities of each way prevent them from being run together by those who, in their religious practice, want "to be all things" and by certain specialists who, in their interpretations, claim that all religions are saying the same thing. In a University of Chicago address, given just before his death, Paul Tillich hoped for an end to the time of "a religion of nonreligion." He looked forward to an era when there would be a reassertion of identifiable form and substance in religious life. The angularity and suchness of Zen and Christianity make each one, in Tillich's phrase, "a religion of the concrete spirit." [1]

To honor the particularity of each is to live in a twofold freedom. The assertion of difference frees us first from thinking we understand religions when we make, all too

170

often, artificial comparisons and analogies. We become free to look at something "as it is," without prejudgments and imposed connections. To admit particularity is to enter into something fully. Before we grasp the connection between the blue mountain and the white cloud, we must know that the mountain is a mountain and the cloud is a cloud. Connection and a sense of *samadhi,* "belonging together," can come only in the midst of knowing that rock, lichen, ridge, and angle are different from vapor, gray-white mass, fleeciness, and motion.

Second, by admitting differences and concentrating on particularities, we can grasp the power of religion rather than attempt to establish truth claims about a tradition or perspective. The insights and symbols of religion, such as Zen emptiness, "morning breeze," "place" and Christian Holy Spirit, "word made flesh," covenant, can function and have power only when special claims are removed. These symbols and insights have their own life and are not deduced from absolute and once-and-for-all truth. As Robert Bellah writes, such powerful terminology, "liberated from its ghetto location in a special group, is released to play its role in the general psychic life." [2]

In the West, we have so often been told that one particular way contains the truth in religion. Many preachers and theologians, moreover, have urged us not to look beyond our Western roots, but to find all our spiritual and psychic needs fulfilled in one tradition. What truth claims have been lavished on certain biblical texts! "We are of God. Whoever knows God listens to us, and he who is not of God does not listen to us. By this we know the spirit of truth and the spirit of error (1 John 4:6)." Proponents of a conservative Roman Catholic view, or of a Protestant evangelical persuasion (or of Islamic conviction), will often try to end attempts to reach beyond their traditions by some such expression as, "A person who really knows *this* religion knows all religions." But today many of us are making another statement, "A person who knows only one religion does not really know any." [3] Truth is being spoken to us today—about ourselves, God, and the world—equivocally, with many equal voices. We cannot cling to statements and perspectives which exclude and restrict; we need, rather, those which include and stretch our horizon. The words in the Revelation to John, though having a historical and particular meaning, fall on many a deaf ear: "I warn everyone who hears the words of the prophecy of this book: If anyone adds to them, God will add to him the plagues described in this book, and if anyone takes away from the words of the book of this prophecy, God will take away his share of the tree of life and in the holy city, which are described in this book (Rev. 22:18–19)."

The respecting of differences and particularities calls into question, for many of us, any claim of absoluteness or triumphalism. Gregory Baum, a Roman Catholic theologian, writes: "A way of announcing God's Word in Jesus must be found which does not devour other religions but actually makes room for the multiple manifestation of God's grace." [4] Our life is many-splendored, and multiple sources are available to us in our quest for value and understanding. As Q. Aurelius Symmachus said in his famous fourth-century controversy with Saint Ambrose: "The heart of so great a mystery cannot ever be reached by following one road only." [5]

A Buddhist insight holds great value for many of us as we deal with the claims of absoluteness made by particular religions. It can be said that the goal of the religious life is not to strive for "the truth" and then to proclaim it widely—especially to nonbelievers—but rather to withdraw from illusion. In "backing out" of attachment to and claims of superiority one begins the road to *nirvana.* To be affixed, to make absolute statements about, to be exclusively defined by one's own religious perspective—these may well be the most destructive illusions from which we must retreat.

So, no absolute truth for many of us today. But there must be that quality which can be called "truth for me." In this time of new possibilities, I find that I may look around with "luminous fish eyes," as many radical polytheists are urging. Nonetheless, I must ask about each thing I see, "Is it true for me?" I must ask if it makes sense to me and whether or not it can become, productively, though painstakingly, a part of my way. I know, personally, I will continue to be an experimenter, taking risks and making mistakes, for, as Tagore says, "If you close your door against all errors, you exclude the truth." [6] But the end of searching and experimentation is, for me, connected with the Hebrew word for truth, *'emeth.* The word signifies a "reality which is solid," which has the connotations of being trustworthy and valid through reason and experience. [7] A word from yet another tradition also characterizes my search. Although there are many Arabic words that can be translated as "truth," Islamic scholars agree that perhaps the most significant is *sidq,* which means the truth which a believer makes for himself—that which he "does" in the rounds of duty, work, decision, and play. [8]

In discovering where insight lies for me, I have moved away from a predominately Greek idea of truth, expressed in the traditional word *alēthia.* The word implies that truth is some high, final, inert principle, standing above all other assertions. Truth means for me, rather, a guide through the intricacies and ambiguities of life, a way of finding personal integration, and a source for action and practice. The fact that it is not categorical and objective does not make this new truth less than very truth and life for me. In making the shift, I have followed, in some sense, Ernst Troeltsch's urging to "overcome history with history." [9] Truth is something of my own making and doing, arising from my own cultural and psychic history, and I use this new insight to overcome an older proclamation of truth, so often triumphantly set forth and laid before me.

My quest for this kind of truth is being fulfilled through the particularities and relationship of Zen and Christianity. Like two prisms, they have refracted different light on the sense of personal value and relationship to others. Different though Zen and Christianity may be, the double illumination has not produced for me contrasting glares or an inharmonious spectrum. As I try to understand how the light of one relates to the light of the other in me, I discover something deeper, namely, that I need the brightness of each, whatever the differences.

I am not claimed by such myriad of perspectives that I find myself, as others today say for themselves, living in a world the center of which is everywhere and the circumference nowhere. My life has a circumscription, set forth by these two traditions. The task for me, in this age of new possibilities—again in the words of a Zen master—is, "Be limitless within your limits."

Meaning in relationship

On a recent winter morning, I divided the hours between reading Hans W. Frei, *The Eclipse of Biblical Narrative: A Study in 18th and 19th-Century Hermeneutics,* and doing zazen. Hans Frei is a friend and former colleague, and I enjoyed being in his presence again. I reveled in the unfolding of his theological argument and in the intricacies of his scholarly work. But I also needed to move away from argument and subtleties—and theories of hermeneutics—to a "place" of no words, no distinctions, and no-mind. The time of thinking, concentration of eyes on printed words, responding in body movement to the unfolding of a point of view ended and I entered a time when I was "letting go," when my eyes were half open and dimly focused on the floor, and when my body was motionless.

Another day began by listening to J. S. Bach, "Singet dem Herrn ein neues Lied!", "Sing unto the Lord a New Song," with orchestra and the full Bach sound. Just when the chorale ended, my students arrived and we began our daily work in a special course entitled "Zen Discipline." We started by chanting the Vedic "Om"—a practice which has many meanings, but is principally conceived to be a vocal expression of the reality of interconnection. The chant is also a reminder of Zen's Indian background. I delighted in Bach's harmonies and development, in the imaginative and engulfing form of psalmody entering my ears, mind, and spirit, and in the wondrous contrasts of range and volume. And, yet, I moved into "Om"—where there was no melody, where there were no references to doctrines in poetry, where I was emptying myself rather than being filled, and where there was repetition rather than progression and development.

The differences between reading Hans Frei and doing zazen and listening to "Singet dem Herrn" and chanting "Om" are vast. Some similarities there may be—one can get lost in Bach and "Om," but the sense of immersion hardly compares, given the symbols, references, and sound of each. I did not think of zazen while reading Hans Frei, nor did I flashback to hermeneutics while counting breaths. And I did not anticipate "diaphragm origin" while listening to Bach, nor did I recall harmonics while trying to be centered in "Om." On those two mornings, I went from one thing to another.

How can one practice and participate in such different things? When Wang Yang-ming was accused in the sixteenth century of contradicting himself with different teachings, he referred to the art of the doctor and said that different pills were used for different illnesses.[10] But there is more to following different ways than prescribing different remedies for different conditions and needs. Zen and Christian can be pursued because the true immersion in one, as mentioned at the end of chapter one, leads a person down deep into an understanding of self, others, and the world. From that place of depth in a particular way, one can be propelled out, as if one had landed on a springboard, to other understandings. My tea-master friend of the opening chapter, offering traditional tea ceremony at a place in the mass, discovered in his authentic act an understanding and sympathy for Roman Catholicism.

But another way, enabling me to participate in different perspectives and practices, is to understand the problem of self-identity. At this point, becoming more philosophical, a deep acknowledgment is made to the thought of Georg W. F. Hegel.[11] I know who I am when I know that I am related to something "other" than what I am. I always know myself in the presence of something else. I am a collection of opposites—active and quiet, yin and yang, assertive and reticent, Zen and Christian. As Heraclitus said, "That which opposes fits." It is impossible to conceive of myself as just a college professor of Western religion, a minister who preaches at village churches and at memorable Christmas carol services in a neo-Gothic chapel, teaches courses on the Puritan tradition, reads Hans Frei's book on biblical narrative, or listens to Bach's "Sing unto the Lord a New Song." Nor can I conceive of myself as being just the teacher of Zen who does zazen, practices cross-country skiing as a body-mind discipline, joins a Kyoto temple, memorizes parts of the *Diamond Sutra,* or chants "Om." "Each 'other' becomes (or is) a 'self' to itself, and each 'self' becomes (or is) an 'other' to another 'self.' This is what 'individuals' are." [12] As Wallace Stevens says: "Nothing is itself taken alone. Things are because of inter-relations or interactions." [13] Only when I see my life lived between polar opposites or contraries, do I know who I am. Such a contrary or polar opposite, as Thomas J. J. Altizer states, "is an opposite in character or in nature, or in position or direction, which is integral to or inherent in its own opposite, and is so continually, and in a never-changing manner and mode." [14] I find Zen and Christianity so related in me—"continually, and in a never-changing manner and mode." As a Christian I know myself in the "other" of Zen, and as a Zen person I know myself in the "other" of Christian faith.

If I am known in the other, I am always ready to go toward it. In his discourse on logic, Hegel speaks of two points or positions, A and B, which could be, for me, Zen and Christian. "They are *directly* connected . . . their con-nection is this, that determinant being has *passed over* into otherness, something into other, and something is just as much an other as the other itself is." [15] Hegel redefines the problem of identity. Instead of using the classic formula that A is A, Hegel prefers a double negative, as expressed in the phrase A is not non-A. The double negative, for Hegel, implies that A has gone to B in order to understand the meaning of A and has returned. Hegel calls to our attention that identity always and necessarily includes dif-ference. I find myself always going to the other in order to know who I am. As a believing Christian I am ready to make the journey to Zen; and as a practicing Zen person I am ready to journey to Christian perspectives. I am always "leaning" toward the other. I am like a two-stringed instrument, to use John Dunne's figure, the first string plucked resonating with the other and the second resonating with the first.

So, for true understanding of myself, I must be ready to go to something else and include it within me. A modern Christian saying is, "If you are willing to die for your faith, you must be also willing to die from it." The Buddhist insight of *anatta,* or no-self, also illuminates the matter. We must practice no-self in connection with what we are at one time and place in order to go to something other than what we are and thereby become the fuller selves we should be. We can know that this dialectical understanding of identity is working if, in our conception of ourselves, something has changed. Have we been enlarged? Are we more realistic about and truer to needs and leanings within ourselves? Or, as Hegel would put it, do we have authentic rather than specious freedom?

My religious life, then, consists not of giving myself exclusively to one point of view or another, but rather in acknowledging the claim that two perspectives have upon me and in relating them. Each remains distinctive and separate. As mentioned in the last chapter, Christianity is not "made into Zen" or Zen Christianized. With all their particularities and differences, the two are caught up in me, as I am caught up in them. Zen and Christianity cannot be compared, but they can meet—in my life and experience. They are related in me by my journey from one to the other and back again. They are not forced together and made something other than what they are. They are together in me because of the journey between. The *Gospel According to Thomas* in Saying 22 reads:

Shall we, then, being children,
enter the Kingdom? Jesus said to them:
When you make the two one . . .
Then you shall enter.[16]

To enter a kingdom is to make a journey—and to make a
true journey is to keep the two in me. They are joined in
me, but I live with the opposites or the binaries as I honor
the uniqueness of each perspective.

Robert Bellah reminds us that our "great summary symbols," such as God, Being, Life, are neither subjective nor
objective, nor cosmological, nor psychological in their
principal meaning. "Rather, they are relational symbols
that are intended to overcome . . . dichotomies of ordinary
conceptualization and bring together the coherence of the
whole of experience."[17] God is known to me as compassion and love. God is known as the giver of all possibilities,
the tap root in the bottom of the lotus pond which makes
possible all the diversities of religion in the world. But
God is especially known as that power in my life which
enables me to relate the Christian concern for "being" with
the Zen insistence on "nonbeing." True relationality does
not place one over the other. I would disagree with Paul
Tillich, who argues that "Being precedes nonbeing in on-
tological validity," that "Being 'embraces' itself and nonbeing," and that "Nonbeing is dependent on the being it
negates."[18] Rather, as Japanese Zen philosophers insist,
the *u* of being and the *mu* of nonbeing are on equal foot-
ing.[19] Fullness and emptiness are both present and needed,
and they are to be related, not ranked. God is the relater
and the giver of being, fullness, *u,* and of nonbeing, emptiness, *mu.* The divine life sustains these differences and
tensions within itself and requires me to discover and practice my own form of relationality. God calls me to move
from contradiction to context.

It is at the place where we take this kind of relationship seriously and formidably that we find God. When we give ourselves entirely to arguments about biblical narrative and then practice zazen and when we chant "Om" after entering the realm of a Bach chorale praising the Creator of the psalmists—then there is a chance of being where God is. For, as Nishida Kitaro says, "We always touch the absolute at the place where individuals determine each other."[20] When we honor the differences that claim us and strive to relate them, we are reflecting divine intentionality. By so thinking, believing, and acting, we are living in the mind of God and joining our spiritual and psychological work with God's.

So I live in an ongoing dialectical process because this is the way of knowing myself and of knowing God. I am identified at any moment by that which I am and by that which I am doing, but also by that which is different and other. As one who appreciates theological argument and nuances of words, I also relish no-mind and "wordless doctrine." Fullness and emptiness are my constituent parts. These parts have become, as I think of my needs and reflect on my experience, mutually founding for me. I hold on to the specialness of Zen and the specialness of Christianity. There is a journey between as I respect them in my quest for understanding of self and of God. I can never know everything about each of them, but I do know that what I understand of each must be functioning in me in order to have authentic life.

Delight

In the eruptive days of the late 1960s, French university students fashioned a slogan, appearing on the walls of buildings and on the bridges across the Seine: "Imagination in Power." It is a saying for all times of unrest and questioning. Today's searching spirit about religion needs the help of imagination. Religion is no longer a defined circle of revealed truth, containing the true believers, but, rather, something more subtle and exciting. It involves the ancient and imaginative idea of pilgrimage, of going from one place to another—on the one hand, the sense of departing, moving away from something and, on the other, of returning, crossing back over. To be religious is to anticipate such a journey, to actually take it, and to identify with the perspectives at either end. Religion is connected with the delight over the limitless wisdom that beckons now from this pole and now from that.

But who is such a person who goes from one thing to another and back again? *"Are* you a Christian?" "Are you *really* a Zen Buddhist?" Such questions come as friendly probing or hostile challenge. They reflect a conventional process of judgment and desire for classification which require that yes be given to one or the other, but not both. Yet, the meaning of self, an understanding of truth, and a quest for God are not so reductive as to be rooted in one or the other. To be *just* one or the other can cloud our vision. Indeed it is often in the middle of the passage, or "on the boundary," that one finds illumination cast on central problems. Rather than seeing one's life as unresolved and full of conflict, one sees that journeying produces a boundary wisdom. It is like pausing on a ridge, while climbing out of one valley, before descending to another, and seizing a momentary view of where one has been and where one is going. Journeying and ridge crossing produce a special insight—a kind of revelatory, startling joy. On the boundary, I come to realize that the opposites in me can include each other—that any experience of *mu,* nonbeing and emptiness, does become *u,* being and fullness, and that the fullness of *u* is illusory, unless involving the emptiness of *mu.* In the midst of crossing, I realize that more is happening in me than I had once thought possible.

The boundary experience is of short duration, for I am en route, crossing over to that which awaits me and about to enter it fully. I am leaving that which is a part of me and I am going to that which is also a part of me. Soon I will go back the other way with the same intent. I am teaching Christian ethics and ministering to a Congregational church, but I am also teaching and practicing Zen Buddhism. When I am doing the one, I am fully involved, and likewise with the other. The situation is similar to the human memory process. Within our minds are stored complex, different, contradictory images, which record our myriad experiences. They are thought to be held in a special storage bank, often described in terms of the hologram—a kind of psychic photographic plate over which each element of our experience is spread intact. The diverse elements do not destroy the integrity of the mind or its function, as now one image, or "set," is called upon and now another.

So it is with Zen and Christian. Zazen and prayer, self-power and other power, fresh "morning breeze" and dependence, Hakuin and Edwards are stored in me. It is good to be quiet and sense their presence and to rejoice over this surprise of Zen and Christian in my being. As I go between them, honoring their differences, I meet God, the spirit of life who calls us to make such journeys. And so this special delight becomes also salvation.

> From this stone I watch the mountains,
>   hear the stream . . .
> I return, a basket brimmed
>   with peaches on my arm.
>
> *Genko*

> For where your treasure is, there will
> your heart be also.
>
> *Matt. 6:21*

Notes

1. Paul Tillich, *A History of Christian Thought: From Its Judaic and Hellenistic Origins to Existentialism,* ed. Carl E. Braaten (New York: Simon & Schuster, 1972), p. xxxiv.

2. Robert N. Bellah, *Beyond Belief: Essays on Religion in a Post-Traditional World* (New York: Harper and Row, 1970), p. 233.

3. Paul Misner, "Two Ecumenisms of Friedrich Heiler," *Andover Newton Quarterly* 15 (March 1975) : 238–49.

4. Gregory Baum, *Religion and Alienation: A Theological Reading of Sociology* (New York: Paulist Press, 1975), p. 195.

5. Robert L. Slater, *World Religions and World Community* (New York: Columbia University Press, 1963), p. 274.

6. *Wind Bell* 9, no. 1 (Winter 1970): 43.

7. Arend T. van Leeuwen, *Christianity in World History: The Meeting of the Faiths of East and West,* trans. H. H. Hoskins (New York: Charles Scribner's Sons, 1964), p. 47.

8. "Talking Points from Books," *Expository Times* 86, no. 2 (November 1974): 33. Elaborating a point from W. Cantwell Smith.

9. Ernst Troeltsch, *The Absoluteness of Christianity and the History of Religions,* trans. David Reid (Richmond, Va.: John Knox Press, 1971), p. 12.

10. Paul Wienpahl, *Zen Diary* (New York: Harper & Row, 1970), p. 41.

11. Particularly to *Wissenschaft der Logik, Science of Logic,* trans. A. V. Miller (New York: Humanities Press, 1969). And to discussions with colleagues Mark C. Taylor and Frederick E. Sontag.

12. Wei Wu Wei, *The Tenth Man* (Hong Kong: Hong Kong University Press, 1967), p. 79.

13. Wallace Stevens, *Opus Posthumous,* ed., intro. Samuel F. Morse (New York: Alfred A. Knopf, 1957), p. 163.

14. Thomas J. J. Altizer, *The Self-Embodiment of God* (New York: Harper & Row, 1977), p. 17.

15. Hegel, *Science of Logic,* pp. 125–26. Mark C. Taylor, "Toward an Ontology of Relativisim," *Journal of the American Academy of Religion* 46, no. 1 (March 1978), and *Journeys to Selfhood: Hegel and Kierkegaard* (Berkeley: University of California Press, 1980), especially chapter 5 "Structures of Spirit."

16. A. Guillaumont et al., trans., eds. *The Gospel According to Thomas: Coptic Text Established and Translated* (New York: Harper and Brothers, 1959), p. 17.

17. Bellah, *Beyond Belief,* p. 202.

18. Paul Tillich, *Systematic Theology* (Chicago: The University of Chicago Press, 1951), 1: 189; and *The Courage to Be* (New Haven: Yale University Press, 1952), pp. 34, 40.

19. Abe Masao, "Non-Being and *Mu:* The Metaphysical Nature of Negativity in the East and in the West," *Religious Studies* 11, no. 2 (June 1975) : 181–92.

20. Nishida Kitaro, *Fundamental Problems of Philosophy,* trans. David A. Dilworth (Tokyo: Monumenta Nipponica, Sophia University, 1970), pp. 28–29.

Index